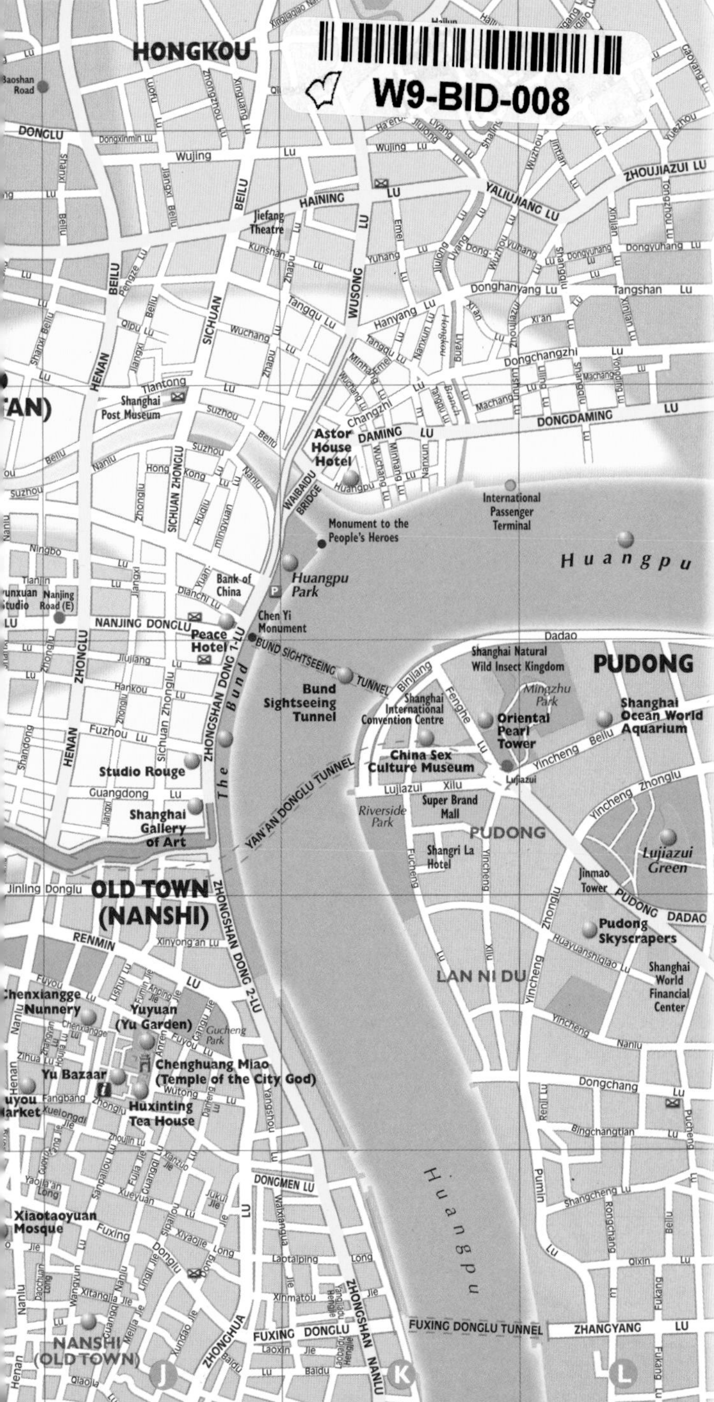

HONGKOU
W9-BID-008
PUDONG
OLD TOWN (NANSHI)
LAN NI DU
Huangpu
Huangpu Park
Monument to the People's Heroes
Astor House Hotel
International Passenger Terminal
Bank of China
Chen Yi Monument
Peace Hotel
Bund Sightseeing Tunnel
The Bund
Shanghai Natural Wild Insect Kingdom
Mingzhu Park
Shanghai International Convention Centre
Oriental Pearl Tower
Shanghai Ocean World Aquarium
China Sex Culture Museum
Super Brand Mall
Riverside Park
Shangri La Hotel
Lujiazui Green
Jinmao Tower
Pudong Skyscrapers
Shanghai World Financial Center
Studio Rouge
Shanghai Gallery of Art
Shanghai Post Museum
Jiefang Theatre
Chenxiangge Nunnery
Yuyuan (Yu Garden)
Gucheng Park
Chenghuang Miao (Temple of the City God)
Yu Bazaar
Huxinting Tea House
Xiaotaoyuan Mosque
NANSHI (OLD TOWN)
NANJING DONGLU
ZHONGSHAN DONG 1-LU
ZHONGSHAN DONG 2-LU
YAN'AN DONGLU TUNNEL
FUXING DONGLU TUNNEL
PUDONG DADAO
DONGDAMING LU
ZHOUJIAZUI LU
WUSONG LU
WAIBAIDU BRIDGE
J
K
L

Fodor's

Shanghai's 25Best

by Christopher Knowles
and George McDonald

Fodor's Travel Publications
New York • Toronto
London • Sydney • Auckland
www.fodors.com

How to Use This Book

KEY TO SYMBOLS

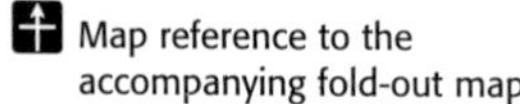

- Map reference to the accompanying fold-out map
- Address
- Telephone number
- Opening/closing times
- Restaurant or café
- Nearest rail station
- Nearest subway (Metro) station
- Nearest bus route
- Nearest riverboat or ferry stop
- Facilities for visitors with disabilities
- Other practical information
- Further information
- Tourist information
- Admission charges: Expensive (more than 50RMB) Moderate (20–50RMB) Inexpensive (20RMB or less)
- Major Sight
- Minor Sight
- Walks
- Excursions
- Shops
- Entertainment and Nightlife
- Restaurants

This guide is divided into four sections
• Essential Shanghai: An introduction to the city and tips on making the most of your stay.
• Shanghai by Area: We've broken the city into seven areas, and recommended the best sights, shops, entertainment venues, nightlife and restaurants in each one. Suggested walks help you to explore on foot. Farther Afield takes you beyond the center.
• Where to Stay: The best hotels, whether you're looking for luxury, budget or something in between.
• Need to Know: The info you need to make your trip run smoothly, including getting about by public transportation, weather tips, emergency phone numbers and useful websites.

Navigation In the Shanghai by Area chapter, we've given each area its own color, which is also used on the locator maps throughout the book and the map on the inside front cover.

Maps The fold-out map accompanying this book is a comprehensive street plan of Shanghai. The grid on this fold-out map is the same as the grid on the locator maps within the book. We've given grid references within the book for each sight and listing.

Contents

Introducing Shanghai

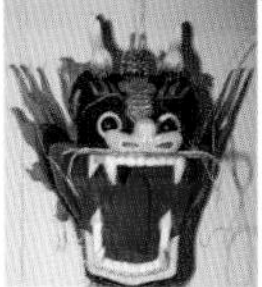

One of the world's great cities, Shanghai is China's dynamic window on the future. A dazzling hybrid of old and new, East and West, communist and capitalist, Shanghai is in the constant throes of reinvention. Prepare to be wowed.

The Shanghainese themselves would likely tell you that Shanghai is the fastest-changing city in the world—and that's before the city has properly hit its stride.

A blend of huge size, a vast and densely packed population, a swirl of fuming traffic, plus a here-today-gone-tomorrow approach to almost everything can make this a hard city to get a handle on. The city's commitment to its past (the Bund, the French Concession) and its future (Pudong) creates a sensation of time moving in two directions, while a frenetically busy population of white-collar workers and the industrious middle classes generate a blur of activity that seldom slows. Shanghai is rarely, if ever, unexciting.

But if you slow the pace yourself to wander through the leafy lanes of the French Concession or track down the city's art deco heritage, you can put the brakes on this fast-moving metropolis and sample its more sedate side. And when you are ready for a further lift, you can speed to one of the highest observation towers in the world for extraordinary views over this breathtaking city. If the view across China's city-of-the-future really takes you, some stratospheric hotels offer round-the-clock panoramas as standard.

Shanghai has some of China's top sights, from the Shanghai Museum to the Bund and the skyscrapers of Pudong. And in its quest to blow the socks off other cities in China, food, drink and entertainment have also received due attention. Shanghai's bars, restaurants and nightclubs are among the most inventive in the land.

Facts + Figures

- **The population of Shanghai is estimated to be around 20 million.**
- **The city generates 5 percent of the nation's annual gross domestic product.**
- **There are some 45,000 taxis in the city.**

HIGH SOCIETY

Around 30 years ago, the Park Hotel, on Nanjing Lu, was the tallest building not just in Shanghai, but in the country. That seems hard to believe now, when the Park Hotel is dwarfed by skyscrapers. Across the Huangpu River, in Pudong, are some of the tallest edifices in the world. Among them is the Oriental Pearl Tower, the tallest such tower in Asia.

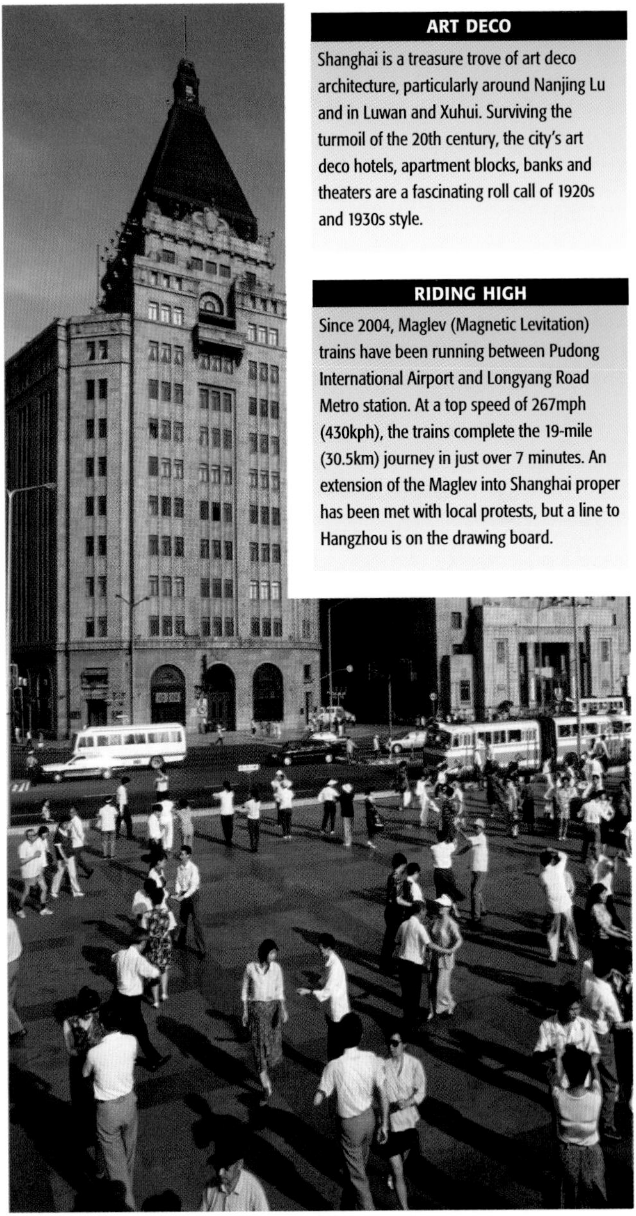

ART DECO

Shanghai is a treasure trove of art deco architecture, particularly around Nanjing Lu and in Luwan and Xuhui. Surviving the turmoil of the 20th century, the city's art deco hotels, apartment blocks, banks and theaters are a fascinating roll call of 1920s and 1930s style.

RIDING HIGH

Since 2004, Maglev (Magnetic Levitation) trains have been running between Pudong International Airport and Longyang Road Metro station. At a top speed of 267mph (430kph), the trains complete the 19-mile (30.5km) journey in just over 7 minutes. An extension of the Maglev into Shanghai proper has been met with local protests, but a line to Hangzhou is on the drawing board.

A Short Stay in Shanghai

DAY 1

Morning Start with breakfast or a coffee at the **Bund 12 Café** (▷ 66) for a taste of prewar Shanghai, then walk along **the Bund** (▷ 58) and the waterfront, looking over to Pudong.

Mid-morning Head for **Yuyuan** (Yu Garden; ▷ 74) in the Old Town, then relax over a pot of Chinese tea in the Huxinting Tea House (▷ 70–71, 79) or the Old Shanghai Tea House (▷ 79).

Lunch Aim for the **Nan Xiang** (▷ 79) for servings of Chinese *xiaolong-bao* (dumplings; ▷ 66), but you may have to wait in line. Or sample one of the Chinese snacks at the plentiful stalls in the **Yuyuan Bazaar** (▷ 76).

Afternoon Wander the narrow streets of the **Old Town** (▷ 72–73), with their popular dumpling restaurants and antiques and jewelry shops.

Mid-afternoon Stroll through **People's Square** (▷ 38–39) and the neighboring **Renmin Park** (▷ 40). Take in the outstanding bronzes, porcelain and paintings in the **Shanghai Museum** (▷ 42–43).

Dinner Have a table reserved on the terrace of **M on the Bund** (▷ 66) for dramatic Pudong night-time views.

Evening Catch an acrobatics performance at the **Shanghai Centre Theatre** (▷ 50), followed by drinks in a French Concession bar (▷ 31).

DAY 2

Morning Have breakfast at the Austrian-themed **Vienna Café** (▷ 32), before visiting **Tianzifang** (▷ 28) to explore its small shops and appealing *shikumen* architecture.

Mid-morning Explore more of the stylish **French Concession** (▷ 24–25), before taking the Metro to Lujiazui to climb to the observation decks of either the **Jinmao Tower** (▷ 94–95) or the **Shanghai World Financial Center** (▷ 95).

Lunch Enjoy a memorable meal at **Jade on 36** (▷ 97), in Tower Two of the Pudong Shangri-La.

Afternoon Go for a cruise on the **Huangpu River** (▷ 60–61), passing through the port area as far as the confluence with the Yangtze River.

Dinner Head to **Xintiandi** (▷ 44) to explore the sights and peruse the shops before dining at **T8** (▷ 51), but make sure you reserve a table. After your meal, have a drink in a Xintiandi bar or stroll through the surrounding streets.

Evening Take the Metro to **People's Square** (▷ 38–39) for a drink in **Barbarossa** (▷ 50) and enjoy some staggering night-time views.

Top 25

Around Suzhou Creek ▷ 56–57 Former consulates and grand old Shanghai mansions.

The Bund ▷ 58–59 Shanghai's splendid embankment is lined with renovated 1920s buildings.

Duolun Lu Cultural Street ▷ 84–85 A historic street, lined with shops and old houses.

Yuyuan ▷ 74 The finest classical garden in Shanghai and the city's most popular tourist sight.

Xujiahui Cathedral ▷ 29 Catholic cathedral easily recognizable by its twin spires and redbrick facade.

Xintiandi ▷ 44 A glamorous collection of shops, entertainment venues and restaurants in restored and rebuilt traditional *shikumen* houses.

Urban Planning Exhibition Hall ▷ 37 Intriguing museum showing the Shanghai of the future.

Tianzifang ▷ 28 Fascinating warren of alleyways, *shikumen* housing, small shops and studios.

Soong Qing-Ling's Residence ▷ 27 The home of Sun Yat-sen's widow is an attractive European villa dating from the 1920s.

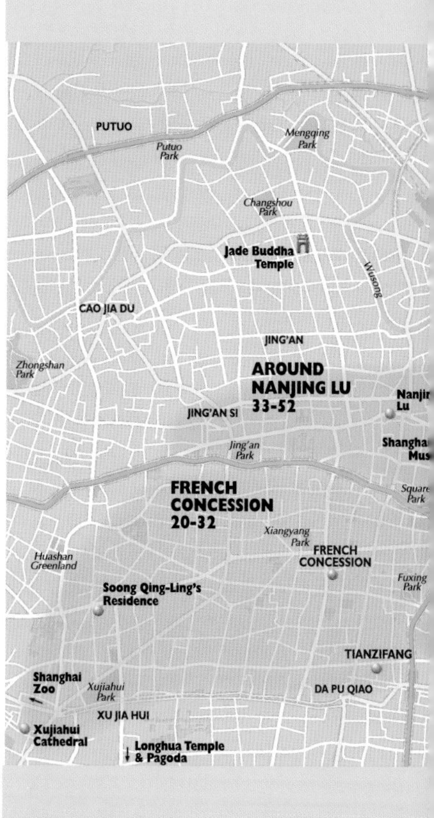

Shanghai Zoo ▷ 104 Pandas, tigers and other creatures in one of the city's greenest parklands.

Shanghai Museum ▷ 42–43 World-class modern museum dedicated to Chinese arts and crafts.

Shanghai Art Museum ▷ 41 The city's foremost art gallery displays Chinese art in the former race club.

These pages are a quick guide to the Top 25, which are described in more detail later. Here they are listed alphabetically, and the tinted background shows which area they are in.

French Concession and Markets ▷ 24–25 Leafy neighborhood with great shopping, as well as sights.

Huangpu Riverboat Tour ▷ 60–61 Get a different perspective of the city from the water.

Huxinting Tea House ▷ 70–71 The familiar building from Blue Willow pattern china.

Jade Buddha Temple ▷ 102–103 Shanghai's most famous temple, with two jade Buddhas.

Longhua Temple and Pagoda ▷ 26 Beautifully restored active temple complex.

Lu Xun Park ▷ 86 Park dedicated to modernist writer Lu Xun.

Nanjing Lu ▷ 36 Shanghai's most famous shopping street, partly pedestrianized.

Old Town ▷ 72–73 Enclave packed with traditional tenement houses and street markets.

Oriental Pearl Tower ▷ 92–93 This familiar tower has become a symbol of Shanghai.

Peace Hotel ▷ 62 Art deco Shanghai's greatest surviving monument is being renovated.

Renmin Park ▷ 40 Pleasant, tranquil space with museums and a pond, right in the heart of the city.

Pudong Skyscrapers ▷ 94–95 The Manhattan of Shanghai is growing new high-rises every year.

People's Square ▷ 38–39 The bustling heart of Shanghai, ringed by modern towers.

Shopping

Shopping is a passion of the Shanghai Chinese. If mainland China has a shopping mall, it has to be Shanghai. From clothing markets and trendy boutiques to swish department stores and mega-malls, the city is at the forefront of the nation's consumer drive.

Nanjing Lu

Nanjing Lu is mainland China's most famous shopping street. While it is particularly touristy in parts, its western section, toward Jing'an Temple, has more style and a larger range of up-to-the-minute department stores. Much of the eastern end of Nanjing Lu has been transformed into a pedestrians-only precinct, which has made shopping there convenient, but this also draws in crowds of out-of-town sightseers. Nanjing Lu is no longer the unchallenged colossus it once was, however, and it has to work increasingly hard to hold its own.

Other Major Streets

Huaihai Zhonglu, in the French Concession, is Nanjing Lu's stylish competitor. North of central Huaihai Zhonglu are several small roads—Changle Lu and Xinle Lu among them—lined with fashionable boutiques for clothes and shoes. Tianzifang (▷ 28) is a lovely warren of alleys devoted to small artist studios, jewelry shops, clothing stores and cafés. Xintiandi (▷ 44) has a popular retail component. The

NEW AREAS

More major shopping zones are opening up. The most important of these is on the Pudong side of the Huangpu River. This area has had a difficult time establishing itself, and some shops have either closed or had to diversify their marketing strategies to cope. However, it seems the continual influx of new residents into the area, and the fact that many of the commuters who work here are among the best-paid in the city, is ensuring its future. The New Shanghai Shopping City mall here is a sign of how things are developing.

Traditional shops and markets attract as much attention as chic malls

Shop for exotic or everyday items in a rapidly growing range of outlets

Old Town's Yuyuan area (▷ panel, below) is great for souvenirs and collectibles. Pudong is home to some monster-malls, but is generally uninspiring for shopping, although this could change in the future (▷ 10, panel). The 50 Moganshan Road Art District (▷ 48) also has a number of trendy shops. More staid Fuzhou Lu is noted for its culturally oriented shops, selling antiques, old books and fine art items.

Department Stores

In addition to individual shops and boutiques, Nanjing Lu hosts several of Shanghai's most notable department stores, shopping malls and supermarkets, among them the New World department store (▷ 48), Shanghai Number One department store, the Plaza 66 mall (▷ 48) and the Wellcome Supermarket (▷ 49). Streets running off Nanjing Lu add to its allure, with superior shopping malls like Raffles City (▷ 49). Huaihai Zhonglu also has several top department stores, including Hong Kong Plaza, Times Square and the Parkson Department Store.

Markets

Shanghai's many street markets are both a resource for reasonably priced goods, and even some bargains, and an attraction in their own right, filled with local atmosphere. Some of the best are in the Old Town.

YUYUAN AREA

Although the rather touristy area in and around the Yu Garden in the Old Town cannot be considered a shopper's paradise in the way that some of the main shopping streets are, in some respects it is more popular with visitors. This is where you can find no end of antiques, arts and crafts, traditional medicines, souvenirs, and all kinds of minor commodities. Most of these go for reasonable prices—but in most cases only after the purchaser has bargained with great tenacity. The crowds that gather here to peruse, bargain and buy are, if anything, more densely packed than those elsewhere.

Shopping by Theme

Whether you're looking for a department store, a quirky boutique, or something in between, you'll find it all in Shanghai. On this page shops are listed by theme. For a more detailed write-up, see the individual listings in Shanghai by Area.

ART GALLERIES

50 Moganshan Road Art District (▷ 48)

BOOKS

Chaterhouse (▷ 48)
Garden Books (▷ 31)
Jin Jiang Hotel Bookshop (▷ 31)
Shanghai Foreign Language Bookstore (▷ 49)

DEPARTMENT STORES AND MALLS

Chia Tai Department Store (▷ 97)
Friendship Store (▷ 78)
Hua Lian (▷ 48)
Isetan (▷ 48)
New World (▷ 48)
Plaza 66 (▷ 48–49)
Raffles City (▷ 49)
Shanghai Spring Department Store (▷ 87)
Wal-Mart Supercenter (▷ 97)
Westgate Mall (▷ 49)
Yatai Shenghui Shopping Centre (▷ 97)

ELECTRONICS

Cybermart (▷ 48)

FASHION

Shanghai Fashion Company (▷ 49)

FOOD AND DRINK

City Shop (▷ 48)
Epicure (▷ 31)
Old Shanghai Tea House (▷ 79)
Parkson Grocery (▷ 31)
Shanghai No. 1 Food Store (▷ 49)
Vienna Café (▷ 32)
Wellcome Supermarket (▷ 49)

MARKETS

Dongtai Lu Antiques Market (▷ 78)
Fumin Small Commodities Market (▷ 78)
Fuyou Market (▷ 76)
Hongqixiang Fabric Market (▷ 78)
Huabao Building Antiques Market (▷ 78)
Qipu Market (▷ 87)
Shanghai Old Street (▷ 78)

SOUVENIRS

Blue Shanghai White (▷ 65)
Dongtai Lu Antiques Market (▷ 78)
Eutoria (▷ 87)
Guo Chun Xiang Curiosity Shop (▷ 87)
Madam Mao's Dowry (▷ 31)
Shanghai Jingdezhen Porcelain Artware Store (▷ 49)
Shanghai Museum Shop (▷ 49)
Silk King (▷ 65)
Silk Museum (▷ 78)
Spin (▷ 31)
Yuyuan Bazaar (▷ 76)

TRADITIONAL SHOPS

Chinese Printed Blue Nankeen Exhibition Hall (▷ 31)
Duoyunxuan Art Studio (▷ 48)
Huangshan Tea Co (▷ 31)
Lao Zhou Hu Cheng Chinese Writing Brush and Inkstick Store (▷ 65)
Lei Yung Shang (▷ 48)
Shanghai Jingdezhen Porcelain Artware Store (▷ 49)
Suzhou Cobblers (▷ 65)
Zhang's Textiles (▷ 49)

Shanghai by Night

ghai lights up after with modern pubs, and cocktail bars and ional Chinese opera

Shanghai is a city that lives hard and plays hard. Its historical position as a meeting ground of East and West has always supplied it with an alluring entertainment scene. Nightlife options are expanding almost daily, and Shanghai is probably China's most cutting-edge city.

Traditional to Modern

As soon as darkness falls, the city lights up as jazz clubs, wine bars, clubs, pubs, cocktail bars and live music venues throw open their doors to well-dressed crowds. And there is a growing palette of highbrow entertainment to choose from, with offerings both traditional and modern, Chinese and international: The list includes classical music, opera, theater and dance, as well as spectacular and artistic acrobatics shows.

Quick Change

It can be hard to keep up with the rapid changes that occur in the nightlife scene. Clubs, pubs and other venues come and go with astonishing ease. Even when an establishment survives, it might up sticks and move to a better location along the same street or to a different part of town. Some nightspots do stand the test of time, but it makes sense to check before getting into a taxi or taking the Metro to a particular venue.

LISTINGS

No fewer than four English-language magazines provide visitors and expats with easily accessible information about what's on, and three of them have their own websites. The weekly *SH* magazine covers events, listings, reviews and features about the city, what's on where, and more; its associated website (www.shmag.cn) keeps you up-to-date online. The monthly magazines *That's Shanghai* and *Shanghai Talk* do the same, usually in greater depth but the information is not quite so timely. Finally, there's the bi-weekly *City Weekend* magazine's Shanghai edition, online at www.cityweekend.com.cn.

Eating Out

Shanghai is naturally the best place on earth in which to sample Shanghainese cuisine, which connoisseurs consider to be a version of the Huaiyang (also known as Yangzhou) cuisine of the lower Yangtze delta. Chefs working in these styles have, across hundreds if not thousands of years, added to a rich store of dishes, menus, ingredients and cooking methods.

Shanghai Cuisine

The city's indigenous cuisine has a number of distinctive characteristics. The "drunken" label attached to some classic dishes, for instance drunken chicken (*zuiji*) or drunken crabs (*zuixie*), arises because they are either marinated or cooked in alcohol such as rice wine. Vinegar, particularly the famed vinegar produced in nearby Zhejiang, is another popular ingredient. Sugar is often used as a sweetener, though since it is generally combined with vinegar, alcohol or soy sauce—or all three together—it creates a sweet-and-sour or savory taste. Since the city is so close to the sea, and because it stands on or near to the Huangpu and Yangtze rivers, sea and freshwater fish and crustaceans form a big part of the menu in city restaurants.

International Menus

As befits its status as China's premier international gateway city, Shanghai has indulged itself and its visitors with national cuisine styles from around the world, along with fusion, world, nouvelle and other fancy variations.

CHINESE STYLES

The city is a rapidly growing melting pot of people from around China. Many have brought their own distinctive regional and even local cuisines with them. There is no shortage of restaurants, ranging from chic high-end places to on-street eateries, serving Cantonese, Sichuan, Pekingese and other major cuisines. You'll also find Tibetan, Mongolian, Xinjiang, Taiwanese, and nowadays even Hong Kong and Maccanese (Macau) restaurants.

Shanghai's restaurants are bursting with Chinese, Asian and international flavors

Restaurants by Cuisine

There are restaurants to suit all tastes and budgets in Shanghai. On this page they are listed by cuisine. For a more detailed description of each restaurant, see Shanghai by Area.

CAFÉS

Boonna Café (▷ 32)
Bund 12 Café (▷ 66)
Element Fresh (▷ 51)
Vienna Café (▷ 32)

CHINESE

Afanti Restaurant (▷ 87)
Dongbeiren (▷ 32)
Duck King (▷ 87)
Guyi Hunan Restaurant (▷ 32)
Mei Long Zhen (▷ 51)
Quanjude (▷ 32)
Xiao Shaoxing (▷ 79)

EUROPEAN

A Future Perfect (▷ 32)
Bella Napoli (▷ 51)
Danieli's (▷ 97)
Fest Brew House (▷ 66)
Jean Georges (▷ 66)
M on the Bund (▷ 66)
Sens & Bund (▷ 66)
Vienna Café (▷ 32)

INTERNATIONAL

Ajisen (▷ 66)
Brasil Steakhouse (▷ 51)
Hong Dong Korean Restaurant (▷ 87)
Jade on 36 (▷ 97)
Kathleen's 5 (▷ 51)
Lan Na Thai (▷ 32)
New Heights (▷ 66)
Sasha's (▷ 32)
T8 (▷ 51)
Vedas (▷ 32)

SHANGHAINESE

Bao Luo (▷ 32)
The Grape (▷ 32)
Lao Fandian (Shanghai Old Restaurant; ▷ 79)
Lu Bo Lang (▷ 79)
Lynn (▷ 51)
Nan Xiang (▷ 79)
Shanghai Uncle (▷ 97)
Whampoa Club (▷ 66)

TEA HOUSES

Huxinting Tea House (▷ 79)
Old Shanghai Tea House (▷ 79)

VEGETARIAN

Gongdelin (▷ 51)
Jade Buddha Temple restaurant (▷ 102)
Songyuelou (▷ 79)
Vegetarian Lifestyle (▷ 51)

If You Like...

However you'd like to spend your time in Shanghai, these top suggestions should help you plan your ideal visit. Each sight or listing has a fuller write-up elsewhere in the book.

INTERNATIONAL SHOPPING

Head for Xintiandi (▷ 44) and its trendy boutique shopping.

Isetan (▷ 48) offers department-store class, Japanese style.

For Western eatables and other products, visit City Shop (▷ 48).

Browse through the warren of small shops and boutiques at Tianzifang (▷ 28).

Shopping in Xintiandi (above and top)

TRADITIONAL SHOPPING

Choose from special Chinese teas and teapots at Huangshan Tea Co (▷ 31).

Shanghai Jingdezhen Porcelain Artware Store (▷ 49) sells fine ceramics from the famed Jingdezhen kilns southwest of Shanghai, in Jiangxi Province.

Shop for hand-embroidered silk slippers at Suzhou Cobblers (▷ 65).

Pick up traditional blue-and-white Chinese clothing at the Chinese Printed Blue Nankeen Exhibition Hall (▷ 31).

LOCAL CUISINE

The Grape (▷ 32) serves Shanghai and Yangzhou cuisine in the setting of a former Orthodox church.

Bao Luo (▷ 32) serves plain but authentic Shanghai food.

Singe your taste buds devouring spicy Hunan cuisine at the Guyi Hunan Restaurant (▷ 32).

Indulge in a modern take on Shanghai cuisine at the stylish Lynn restaurant (▷ 51).

Chinese tea (above right); a tasty local dish (right)

The art deco Peace Hotel (below)

CHARACTER HOTELS

The Peace Hotel (▷ 62) is one of the outstanding colonial-era buildings on the Bund.
Mansion Hotel (▷ 110), in the French Concession, is steeped in the memories of Shanghai's 1930s gangster heyday.
Astor House Hotel (▷ 63, 110) dates from the early 19th century and bursts with character.
Old House Inn (▷ 111) is a small hotel that makes up for what it lacks in size with old-fashioned class.
Swathe yourself in the historic charms of the former Morris Estate at the splendid Ruijin Guest House (▷ 111).

HOT AND COOL

Relax with a drink in the effortlessly elegant ambience of Face (▷ 31), a bar in the French Concession.
At Bar Rouge (▷ 65) the well-prepared cocktails are followed by well-crafted DJ sounds.
Dance your socks off and lap up the views at Attica (▷ 65).
Glamour Bar (▷ 65): The name says it all—a glamorous bar, with a great position at the Bund.

y a cocktail at a rt bar (above) or in a memorable batics show (below)

ENTERTAINMENT

Cathay Theatre (▷ 31) offers the best Chinese and international cinema in a 1930s art deco gem of a building.

The Majestic Theatre (▷ 50) stages traditional Chinese opera, music and dance.
Shanghai Conservatory of Music (▷ 31) is a wonderful venue for classical music, both Chinese and Western.
Shanghai Centre Theatre (▷ 50) is the place for enjoying mind-spinning acrobatics performances.

Fuyou Market and Longhua Temple (below)

LOOKING FOR A BARGAIN

Etour Youth Hostel (▷ 109) is a handy and well-presented hostel right on the edge of People's Square.
Boonna Café (▷ 32) comes up trumps with inexpensive coffee and a trendy, casual ambience.
Ajisen (▷ 66) offers diners excellent bowls of spicy Japanese noodles, a photo menu and brisk service.
Shanghai Museum (▷ 42–43) is China's very best museum and it's currently free to visit.
The Bund (▷ 58–59) is Shanghai's top sight and it won't cost you a penny.

SCENT OF SANCTITY

Longhua Temple and Pagoda (▷ 26) is Shanghai's most venerable Buddhist temple and dates back to the Song dynasty.
Xujiahui Cathedral (▷ 29) was founded by Jesuit priests, and is still a stronghold of the Chinese Catholic church.
Jade Buddha Temple (▷ 102) is China's best-known Buddhist Temple.

COLONIAL AIRS AND GRACES

Not everything in the French Concession (▷ 24–25) is French, but enough francophone architecture, parks and broad boulevards survive to give the idea of a certain prewar *je ne sais quoi*.
Soong Qing-Ling's Residence (▷ 27), a 1920s European-style villa, was home to the wife of the founder of modern China, Sun Yat-sen.
Sit down to a meal or a drink at Sasha's (▷ 32) and surround yourself in its historic villa charms.

The popular terrace outside Sasha's bar (right) and a wall painting (above right) in the French Concession

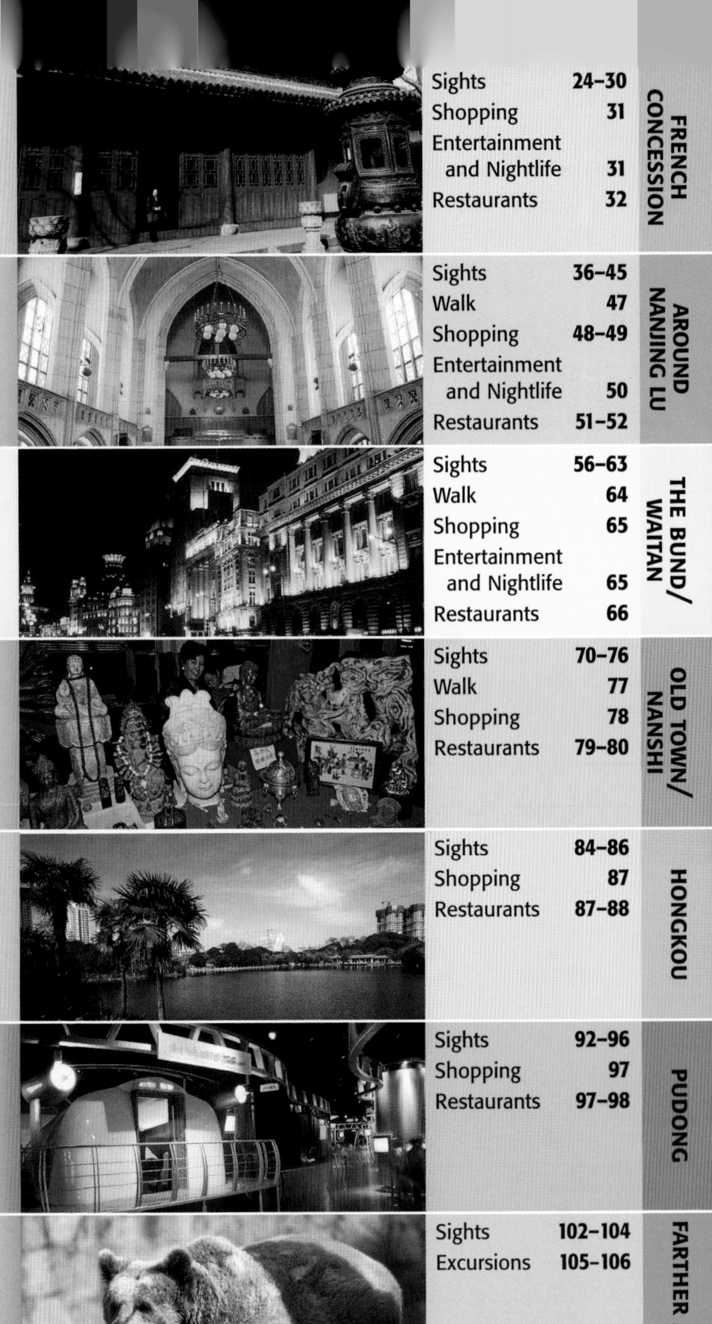

French Concession

The stylish French Concession ranges from art deco apartment blocks, *shikumen* architecture and *lilong* alleys to trendy boutiques, chic restaurants and European-style, tree-shaded streets.

4
5
6
7
8
9
A
B
C
Propaganda Poster Art Centre
Ding Xiang Garden
Soong Qing-Ling's Residence
C Y Tung Maritime Museum
Jiaotong University
Xujiahui Park
Xujiahui Cathedral
XU JIA HUI
Longhua Temple & Pagoda
Nie Er Monument
Shanghai Library
Changshu Road
Hengshan Road
Xujiahui
Huashan Lu
Changle Lu
Anfu Lu
Wuyuan Lu
Fuxing Xilu
Hunan Lu
Gaoyou Lu
Wukang Lu
Yongfu Lu
Tai'an Lu
Huaihai Zhonglu
Taojiang
Dongping Lu
Wulumuqi Beilu
Wulumuqi Zhonglu
Wulumuqi Nanlu
Changshu Lu
Baoqing Lu
Xingguo Lu
Yuqing Lu
Tianping Lu
Kangping Lu
Wanping Lu
Wuxing Lu
Gao'an Lu
Hengshan Lu
Yongjia Lu
Anting Lu
Yueyang Lu
Guangyuan Lu
Jianguo Xilu
Zhaojiabang Lu
Hongqiao Lu
Caoxi Beilu
Tianyaoqiao Lu
Wanping Nanlu
Ziyang Lu
Puxi Lu

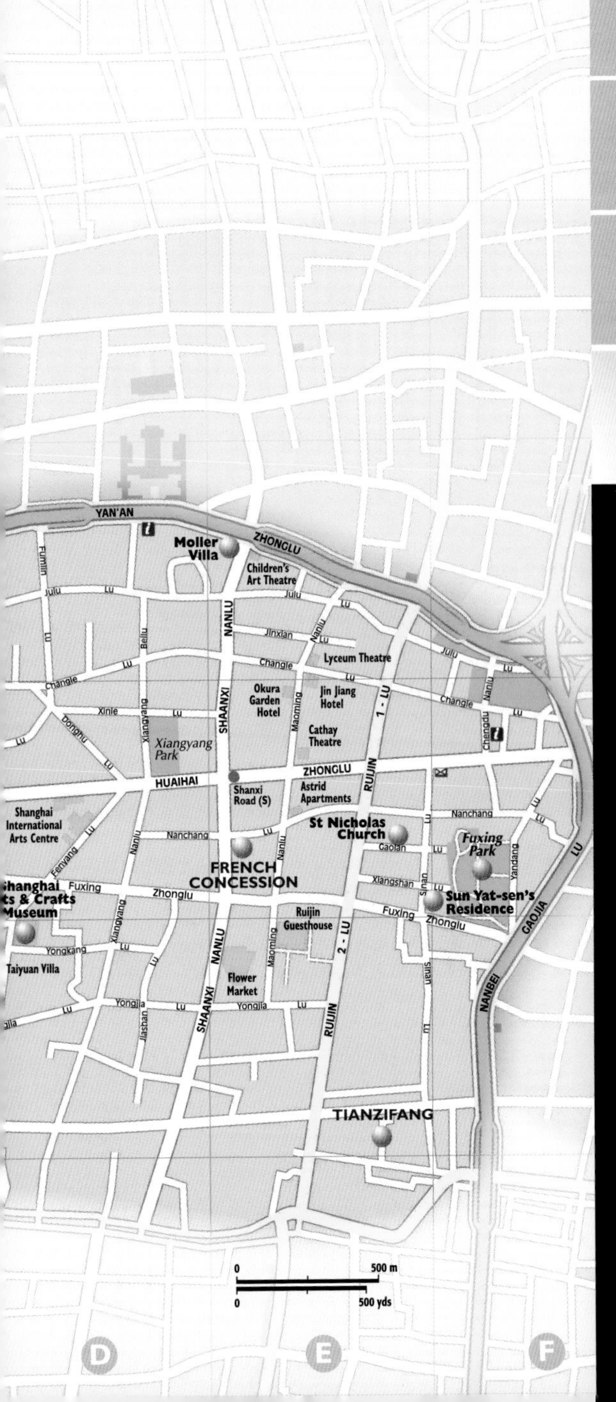
YAN'AN
ZHONGLU
Moller Villa
Children's Art Theatre
Fumin Lu
Julu Lu
Julu Lu
Jinxian Lu
Nanlu
Beijiu
SHAANXI NANLU
Changle Lu
Changle
Lyceum Theatre
Julu
Lu
Changle
Nanlu
Lu
Xinle Lu
Donghu Lu
Okura Garden Hotel
Jin Jiang Hotel
Maoming
RUIJIN 1 - LU
Chengdu
Xiangyang
Xiangyang Park
Cathay Theatre
HUAIHAI
ZHONGLU
Shanxi Road (S)
Astrid Apartments
Shanghai International Arts Centre
Nanchang
St Nicholas Church
Gaolan Lu
Nanchang
Fuxing Park
Yandang
Fenyang
Nanlu
FRENCH CONCESSION
Xiangshan
Sinan Lu
Sun Yat-sen's Residence
Shanghai Arts & Crafts Museum
Fuxing Zhonglu
Ruijin Guesthouse
Fuxing Zhonglu
GAOJIA LU
Yongkang Lu
Xiangyang
Maoming
RUIJIN 2 - LU
Sinan Lu
NANBEI
Taiyuan Villa
SHAANXI NANLU
Flower Market
Yongjia Lu
Yongjia Lu
Jiashan
TIANZIFANG
0
500 m
0
500 yds
D
E
F

French Concession and Markets

HIGHLIGHTS

- Fascinating colonial-era architecture
- Excellent shopping
- Fine restaurants and bars
- Theaters and cinemas
- Small but welcome parks

TIP

- Huaihai Zhonglu, which slices laterally through the French Concession, runs for 3.5 miles (6km). Three Metro stations–Huangpi Road (S), Changshu Road and Shanxi Road (S)–are dotted along it.

Oozing style and sophistication, the French Concession–"Frenchtown"–is Shanghai's most chic area: a classy blend of trendy restaurants, discerning cafés, stylish boutiques, art deco architecture and European-style villas.

France Outre Mer The French Concession lay to the south of the original British Settlement, and to the west of the old Chinese town. Having grown to an area of 4sq miles (10sq km), it refused the invitation to join the Americans and British in forming the International Settlement in 1863. The French Settlement had its own buses and trams, its own electricity and its own judicial system and traffic regulations–and it added spice to the steaming cosmopolitan brew that was Shanghai. Gangsters and revolutionaries, bon-vivants and

Clockwise from the left: Pedestrians on busy Huaihai Zhonglu; a reading room; traditional cloth designs at the Chinese Printed Blue Nankeen Exhibition Hall (▷ 31); the traffic passing along Huaihai Zhonglu; a table set for dinner at Yin Restaurant; enjoying evening drinks at Sasha's (▷ 32)

refugees were attracted to the Concession and by 1930 French residents were easily outnumbered by Americans, Britons and Russians.

Touring the French Concession The heart of the old Concession was Avenue Joffre, today's Huaihai Zhonglu, which is still at least as good a shopping street as the more famous Nanjing Lu (▷ 36). Tianzifang (▷ 28) is excellent for shopping and dining in an attractive *shikumen* environment. Art deco buildings can be found at every turn, from the Jinjiang Hotel to the Cathay Theatre, while other gems—St. Nicholas Church, Ruijin Guest House, the Moller Villa—dot the tree-lined streets. Other standout relics include the grandiose entrance to the east wing of the former French club, Le Cercle Sportif Francais (now part of the Okura Garden Hotel Shanghai, ▷ 112).

THE BASICS

- C7–F7
- Around Huaihai Zhonglu
- Many excellent restaurants
- Shanxi Road (S)
- 10, 42, 911
- None

Longhua Temple and Pagoda

The gates to the temple (left); worshipers inside; a carved lion (right)

THE BASICS

- Off map at A9
- 2853 Longhua Lu
- 6456 6085
- Daily 8–4
- Excellent vegetarian restaurant on premises
- 41, 44, 73, 104, 864
- None
- Inexpensive

HIGHLIGHTS

- Handsome pagoda
- Active temple

TIP

- The best times to visit the temple are at New Year or during one of the festivals: Birthday of the Queen of Heaven (Mar 23), Birthday of Sakyamuni Buddha (Apr 8), Temple Fair (May Day Holiday Week and October National Vacation Week). There are processions and traditional music.

"The ancient temple stands tall and proud, the pagoda towers into the cloud. Willows encircle the river village, Streams are reddened by the blooming peach". From a Tang dynasty poem.

The pagoda Unusually for Chinese pagodas that survive with their associated Buddhist temples, the stupa here rises up beyond the main temple grounds. The pagoda's foundations date from AD977 (Song dynasty), and although the pagoda has certainly been rebuilt many times since then, it retains the architectural features of the Song period. Seven floors and 134ft (41m) high, the pagoda is octagonal and made of wood and brick, with "flying" eaves of gray tile; unfortunately, it cannot be climbed. It stands on the site of another pagoda, thought to have been built during the period known as the Three Kingdoms (AD238–251).

The temple According to legend, the Longhua Temple was founded during the Three Kingdoms period by the king of Wu and Kang Monk Hui, the son of an eminent minister, who was attracted by this marshy area where "the water and the sky were of one color." It is more likely that its earliest construction was during the Five Dynasties period (AD923–979). In any event, the current buildings date from the end of the 19th century, during the final (Qing) dynasty. After years of neglect the temple reopened and there are several dozen monks in residence. The temple and its surroundings are noted for their spring peach blossom.

The front garden (left); a limousine presented to Soong Qing-Ling (right)

Soong Qing-Ling's Residence

The villa of Soong Qing-Ling, widow of Sun Yat-sen, the father of Republican China, paints a charming portrait of a vanished Shanghai era. A visit here gives glimpses of how the wealthy lived during a vital period in China's modern history.

Soong Qing-Ling Born in Shanghai in 1893 to a family whose business was bible printing, Soong Qing-Ling was introduced to Sun Yat-sen through her father's connections with secret societies dedicated to the fall of the emperor. In 1913, on her way home from the US, where she was educated, she met Sun in Japan rallying support for the restoration of the republic he had founded in 1911. She became his secretary and married him in 1915. After Sun's death she became disenchanted with his successor Chiang Kai Shek and went to Moscow, returning to help with the anti-Japanese war effort. After the revolution she held a number of government posts and became a useful symbol for China until her death in 1981.

The residence Soong Qing-Ling's home in Shanghai from 1948 to 1963, in the heart of the French Concession, dates from the 1920s. The house, a European-style villa with a pretty garden, has been maintained as it was on the day that she died. As befits the home of a representative of the people, it is furnished fairly simply, although there is an interesting collection of gifts received from a number of eminent visitors, including a carpet from Mao, and a work in bamboo from Kim Il Sung of North Korea.

THE BASICS

www.shsoong-chingling.com
B8
1843 Huaihai Zhonglu
6474 7183
Daily 9–4.30
Hengshan Road
None
Inexpensive

HIGHLIGHTS

- Lovely prewar villa with period furnishings
- Well-tended European-style garden

Tianzifang

Browsing the shops and cafés in Tianzifang's alleys

THE BASICS

E8
Lane 210, Taikang Lu
Restaurants and cafés
Shanxi Road (S), then taxi
None

HIGHLIGHTS

- *Shikumen* architecture
- Shopping
- Taking a coffee break

TIP

- When visiting the Deke Erh Art Centre, look out for photographer Deke Erh's excellent book (co-written with Tess Johnston), *Art Deco Shanghai*.

Admire Shanghai's alleyway *shikumen* architecture while shopping at some of the city's most creative clothes shops and sipping coffee at trendy cafés. This small tangle of lanes is a great alternative to Shanghai's mega-malls.

***Shikumen* style** Like Beijing's *siheyuan* courtyard architecture, Shanghai's *shikumen* residences are motifs of the city. A marriage of 19th-century British terrace housing and traditional Chinese courtyard architecture, *shikumen* buildings—tucked away in rows down alleys called *lilong*—are low-rise, with two or three floors, and fronted with an often elaborately carved stone lintel, lending the name *shikumen* (stone-surrounded gate). In Tianzifang (also called Taikang Lu Art Street), many of these *shikumen* residences have been converted to boutiques and small shops.

A welcome escape Not as well known as Xintiandi (▷ 44), Tianzifang has a more small-scale and manageable charm that makes a visit a more relaxing experience. Grab a coffee and read a good book at the Deke Erh Art Centre (No. 2, Lane 210, Taikang Lu), on your left as you walk up the main alley. For artists' studios, pop into the International Artists Factory, a modern block on your right, also home to several design outfits and boutiques. Alleys branch off from the main lanes, leading to courtyards and further alleys with small clothes boutiques, jewelry shops and restaurants. For a break, take an outside seat at boho café Kommune (No. 7, Lane 210) and watch the world go by.

The cathedral's ornate ceiling (left) and altar (right)

Xujiahui Cathedral

In a country of Buddhist, Confucian and Taoist traditions that is now officially atheist, perhaps nothing is more surprising than the twin towers of a redbrick neo-Gothic cathedral poking into the sky in the shadow of gleaming skyscrapers.

The Jesuits The influence of Jesuit missionaries was felt in Shanghai from as early as the 16th century. An early convert was one Xu Guangqi, a native of Xujiahui, or "Xu Family Village," which at that time was well outside the original town of Shanghai. Xu, an official in the Imperial library, was baptized Paul. He later bequeathed family land to the Jesuits, where an observatory and cathedral would eventually be constructed. Following persecution of the converts, the first church here became a temple to the god of war; after the Treaty of Nanking (1842), the land was given to the French, and in 1848 a Jesuit settlement was firmly established.

The cathedral The current cathedral of St. Ignatius was built in 1906 with two 165ft (50m) spires and capacity for a congregation of 2,500. The interior includes a number of decorative idiosyncracies that indicate Buddhist influence—melons appear on the nave columns and, along with stylized bats (a Chinese symbol of happiness), in the windows. Outside, gargoyles fringe the roof and a holy grotto has been built in the garden. Severely damaged during the Cultural Revolution, the cathedral is now a busy place of worship.

THE BASICS

A9
158 Puxi Lu
6438 4632
Daily
Xujiahui
3, 42, 50
None
Free
Services Mon–Fri 6am, 7am; Sat 6am, 7am, 6pm; Sun 6am, 8am

HIGHLIGHTS

- European neo-Gothic among the skyscrapers
- Idiosyncratic detail

TIP

- Pop into the nearby Bibliotheca Zi-Ka-Wei (80 Caoxi Beilu) and try to get on the free Saturday tours (2–4pm) of the main Jesuit library room—it's outstanding.

More to See

C.Y. TUNG MARITIME MUSEUM

Wander around historic Jiaotong University before visiting this museum, dedicated to Chinese maritime history.
A8 Jiaotong University Tue–Sun 1.30–5.30 Xujiahui Free

FUXING PARK

A private garden converted in 1908 into a Parisian-style park and pleasantly shaded by Wutong trees, Fuxing Park is a delicious spot for a relaxing stroll.
F7 Fuxing Zhonglu Daily Restaurants Huangpi Road (S) 24 None Free

MOLLER VILLA

Now a hotel, this curious concoction of Gothic towers and spires was home to a Scandinavian shipping magnate.
E6 30 Shaanxi Nanlu 6247 8881 Shanxi Road (S) 42

PROPAGANDA POSTER ART CENTRE

This gallery exhibits a fine collection of political propaganda posters from the Mao era. It's a quirky diversion and a reminder of China's recent radicalism.
B6 Room B-OC, President Mansion, 868 Huashan Lu 6211 1845 Jiangsu Road 93 Moderate

ST. NICHOLAS CHURCH

Just west of Fuxing Park, this 1930s Russian Orthodox Church, now empty, is an attractive feature of Gaolan Lu.
E7 16 Gaolan Lu Huangpi Road (S)

SHANGHAI ARTS & CRAFTS MUSEUM

This museum of traditional Chinese arts and crafts is in an elegant mansion with a beautiful garden.
D8 79 Fenyang Lu 6437 3454 Daily 8.30–4.30 Changshu Road 42 None Inexpensive

SUN YAT-SEN'S RESIDENCE

The house of the father of Republican China has been kept as it supposedly was during his life, simply furnished in a mix of Western and Chinese styles.
F7 7 Xiangshan Lu 6437 2954 Daily 9–4.30 Shanxi Road (S) 2, 17, 24, 36, 42

A grand wooden staircase inside Moller Villa (left); Sun Yat-Sen's Residence (below)

Shopping

CHINESE PRINTED BLUE NANKEEN EXHIBITION HALL
Delightful traditional blue-and-white cloth designs.
D7 No. 24, Lane 637, Changle Lu 5403 7947 Daily 9–5 Changshu Road

EPICURE
Classy wine store.
D7 98 Xinle Lu 5404 7719 Daily 10am–11pm Shanxi Road (S)

GARDEN BOOKS
An airy bookstore selling a range of books and international magazines.
E6 325 Changle Lu 5404 8728 Daily 10–10 Shanxi Road (S)

HUANGSHAN TEA CO
All you need for tea, including ceramics and Yixing teapots.
F7 605 Huaihai Zhonglu 5306 2258 Daily 9am–10pm Huangpi Road (S) 42, 911

JIN JIANG HOTEL BOOKSHOP
A good bookshop within the precincts of the old Jin Jiang Tower.
E7 59 Maoming Nanlu 6472 1273 Shanxi Road (S)

MADAME MAO'S DOWRY
Trendy collectibles from the Cultural Revolution, along with antiques from dynastic China.
D6 207 Fumin Lu 5403 3551 Daily 10–7 Changshu Road

PARKSON GROCERY
A Western-style supermarket taking up one floor of the department store of the same name.
E7 Basement Level, Parkson Department Store, 918 Huaihai Zhonglu 6415 6384 Shanxi Road (S) 42, 126, 911

SPIN
Jingdezhen ceramics with a trendy, modern twist.
D6 Building 3, 758 Julu Lu 6279 2545 Daily noon–10pm Jing'an Temple

Entertainment and Nightlife

BONBON
www.clubbonbon.com
Hip club with international DJs and a devoted crowd.
C7 2nd floor, Yunhai Tower, 1331–1329 Huaihai Zhonglu Daily 8.30pm–late Changshu Road

CATHAY THEATRE
A restored treasure of 1930s art deco, the cinema has three screens that show Chinese and new international films.
E7 870 Huaihai Zhonglu 5404 0415/5404 2095 Shanxi Road (S) 41

CLUB JZ
For late-night modern jazz sounds, Club JZ is one of Shanghai's best; open mic on Monday nights.
C7 46 West Fuxing Road 6385 0269 Daily 9pm–3am Changshu Road

FACE
www.facebars.com
Elegant and much-loved bar in the Ruijin Guest House (▷ 111); a relaxing and civilized option.
E8 118 Ruijin 2-Lu 6466 4328 Daily noon–1.30am Shanxi Road (S)

MANIFESTO
Manifesto is a cool, stylish bar with a popular terrace for summer drinks.
D6 748 Julu Lu 6289 9108 Daily 11am–2am Jing'an Temple

SHANGHAI CONSERVATORY OF MUSIC
Regular performances of classical Chinese and Western music most Sunday evenings.
D7 20 Fenyang Lu 6437 0137, ext. 2166 Shanxi Road (S)

Restaurants

PRICES

Prices are approximate, based on a 3-course meal for one person.
$$$ more than 250RMB
$$ 100–250RMB
$ under 100RMB

A FUTURE PERFECT ($$)
Opening onto a courtyard garden next to the Old House Inn, this lovely restaurant has a winning European menu and a relaxed and stylish vibe.
C6 No. 16, Lane 351 Huashan Lu 6248 8020 Daily 7am–midnight Changshu Road

BAO LUO ($)
Easy to miss but hard to forget, this plain but inviting restaurant serves uncompromisingly traditional Shanghainese cuisine, which is just what the many locals who pile in here, and the visitors who join them, have come to enjoy.
D6 271 Fumin Lu 5403 7239 Daily 11–6 Changshu Road

BOONNA CAFÉ ($)
Great music and coffee in a snug, intimate space.
D7 88 Xinle Lu 5404 6676 Daily 7am–1am Shanxi Road (S)

DONGBEIREN ($)
Fantastically popular Manchurian restaurant with tremendous food, smiling waitresses and a fun, relaxing atmosphere.
E6 1 Shaanxi Nanlu 5228 9898 Daily 11–10 Shanxi Road (S)

THE GRAPE ($$)
In a former church, the service is friendly and the Shanghai and Yangzhou cooking reliable. Try the Yangzhou fried rice, the salt-and-pepper pork chops and the claypot eggplant with vermicelli.
D7 55 Xinle Lu 5404 0486 Daily lunch, dinner 45

GUYI HUNAN RESTAURANT ($–$$)
If you've had enough of Shanghai cuisine's soft flavors, go for the full-on spiciness of the much-enjoyed Hunan dishes at this smart restaurant.
D6 87 Fumin Lu 6249 5628 Daily 11.30am–4pm Jing'an Temple

LAN NA THAI ($$)
Fabulous Thai food and indulgent surroundings just above Face bar (▷ 31), in the Ruijin Guest House (▷ 111).
E8 Building 4, Ruijin Guest House, 118 Ruijin 2-Lu 6466 4328 Daily noon–2.30, 5.30–10.30 Shanxi Road (S)

EXPENSIVE OPTIONS

Always check the cost of dishes that do not have a price on them on the menu. Seasonal dishes, particularly those involving seafoods, can be expensive, even on an otherwise inexpensive menu.

QUANJUDE ($–$$)
Famed across China for its Peking duck, Quanjude –a popular brand from Beijing–has a handy outpost in Shanghai.
E7 4th floor, 786 Huaihai Zhonglu 5403 7286 Daily 11–2, 5–10 Shanxi Road (S)

SASHA'S ($–$$)
A rambling, rose-hued 1920s villa is home to this cool restaurant and bar. There's elegant international dining in an upstairs room, and casual munching on pizzas and sundry snacks in the bar or on the garden terrace.
C7 11 Dongping Lu 6474 6628 Daily 11.30–2, 5.30–10 Changshu Road

VEDAS ($–$$)
With great service, classic dishes and a civilized and attractive ambience, Vedas is probably the city's best Indian restaurant.
C8 550 Jianguo Xilu 6445 3670 Daily 11.30–2, 5.30–11 Hengshan Road

VIENNA CAFÉ ($)
Excellent Austrian-themed café with great food, coffee and an effortless, comforting tempo.
E8 25 Shaoxing Lu 6445 2131 Daily 8–8 Shanxi Road (S)

The frenetic Nanjing Lu shopping street skirts the edge of Shanghai's concentration of governmental and cultural installations around the People's Park and Square.

3
4
5
6
7
8
9
C
D
E
Xinzha Lu
Xikang Lu
Shaanxi Beilu
Xinzha Lu
Taixing Lu
Zhangjiazhai Lu
SHIMEN 2-LU
BEIJING XILU
Nanjing Lu
Shanghai Centre
Nanyang Lu
Majestic Theatre
Nanhui Lu
JING'AN SI
Lilong Architecture
Yuyuan Lu
Jiaozhou Lu
Yuyuan Lu
Changde Lu
Tongren Lu
Wujiang
Nanjing Road (W)
Jing'an Temple
NANJING XILU
Taixing Lu
Beilu
NANJING XILU
Children's Palace
HUASHAN LU
Jing'an Park
Jing'an Temple
Anyi Lu
Shanghai Exhibition Centre
SHAANXI BEILU
Weihai Lu
1-LU
YAN'AN ZHONGLU
Maoming Lu
Ruijin Theatre
SHIMEN
Dagu
0
500 m
0
500 yds

NI CHENG QIAO
(Suzhou Creek)
Wusong
Xinzha Road
Huangpu Theatre
Zhongguo Theatre
BEIJING XILU
BEIJING DONGLU
Grand Brightness Theatre
People's Square
Wusha Monument
Renmin Park
MOCA
Shanghai Art Museum
Shanghai Municipal People's Government
Urban Planning Exhibition Hall
Shanghai Grand Theatre
People's Square
Shanghai Museum
Duoyunxuan Art Studio
Nanjing Road (E)
NANJING DONGLU
NANJING XILU
XIZANG (TIBET ROAD) ZHONGLU
Yifu Theatre
HUANGPU
YAN'AN DONGLU
Gong Theatre
Concert Hall
Square Park
Dazhong Theatre
Huangpi Road (S)
HUAIHAI ZHONGLU
HUAIHAI DONGLU
Dashijie
Huaihai Park
Memorial House of the First National Congress of the Communist Party
Xintiandi
Taipingqiao Park
Laoximen
XIZANG (TIBET ROAD) NANLU
LUWAN
Fuxing Zhonglu
Jianguo Donglu
CHENGDU BEILU
GAOJIA
G
H

Nanjing Lu

Neon lights (left); a flying-saucer-style revolving restaurant tops the Radisson (far right)

THE BASICS

C6–J5
Many excellent restaurants
Nanjing Road (E), People's Square, Nanjing Road (W), Jing'an Temple
5, 20, 37
None

HIGHLIGHTS

- Heart of workaday Shanghai
- Excellent shopping
- Period architecture

TIP

- Nanjing Donglu can be noisy, with huge numbers of shoppers and tourists. If you want to evade the crowds and speed along the pedestrianized length of Nanjing Donglu, jump aboard one of the fun tourist "trains" that travel from the People's Square end to Henan Zhonglu. Tickets are cheap and trains leave regularly.

Starting at the Bund's Peace Hotel, storming through People's Square, and taking shoppers all the way west to the Jing'an Temple, Nanjing Road is Shanghai's most famous thoroughfare.

The past The name commemorates the treaty that, in 1842, gave trading rights to the foreign powers of the era (▷ 124). As Shanghai grew, so did Nanjing Lu, snaking through the heart of the International Settlement to become, at its western end, the Bubbling Well Road (now Nanjing Xilu), named after a well near the Jing'an Temple.

Today Although rivaled by Huaihai Zhonglu for shopping, Nanjing Lu remains Shanghai's pre-eminent thoroughfare, bordered in the east by the Bund and the Huangpu River. Nanjing Donglu (East Nanjing Road) is the liveliest section, especially the pedestrians-only strip between Henan Zhonglu and Xizang Zhonglu—come here at night for a street of dazzling neon, with the illuminated towers of Pudong in the distance. While walking along Nanjing Donglu, keep an eye out for its splendid art deco buildings, including the Peace Hotel (▷ 62). Other historic buildings include the Shanghai No. 1 Department Store and the former Shanghai Sincere Department Store, now housing the East Asia Hotel (▷ 109). Where Nanjing Donglu meets Nanjing Xilu (Nanjing Road West) is the old racecourse grandstand and clock, now home to the Shanghai Art Museum (▷ 41), and the Park Hotel, the tallest building outside the Americas at the time of its construction in 1934.

Exterior of the hall (left); scale models of the city (right)

Urban Planning Exhibition Hall

This fascinating museum (Chengshi Guihua Zhanshiguan), on the eastern end of People's Square, propels visitors into the future by showing them what the city might look like in the year 2020.

What's in a name? They could easily have given this museum a more attractive name, but don't judge it on this basis alone. Begin your odyssey on the mezzanine floor, where a 20-minute film takes you on a whistle-stop tour of 100 years of Shanghai history.

City plans Prepare to be bowled over by the star attraction, a scale model of the city as it is planned to look in the year 2020, so detailed that it takes up the entire third floor. The high-tech displays on the fourth floor turn the spotlight on mammoth construction projects like the Yangshan deep-water port and the Shanghai World Expo site.

Relentless change One rather sad exhibit is of those older areas that are slated for demolition, only to be replaced by soulless modern apartments and office towers. Not all of this will be considered a loss by their current residents, whose wish for more comfortable accommodations will be fulfilled. Yet parts of town that might well be worth saving and refurbishing will disappear, too, and there seems to be nothing to stop the development juggernaut that has already rolled over so many parts of old Shanghai. In partial compensation, there are working re-creations of old shops and tea houses in the museum basement.

THE BASICS

www.supec.org
G6
100 Renmin Dadao
6372 2077
Mon–Thu 9–5, Fri–Sun 9–6 (last ticket one hour before closing)
Museum café
People's Square
40, 71, 123, 574
Moderate
Few

HIGHLIGHTS

- Scale model of Shanghai's 2020 vision
- Top-floor café

TIP

- Take an opera glass or a small pair of binoculars for close-up views of the beautifully detailed scale model of Shanghai in 2020.

People's Square

TOP 25

HIGHLIGHTS

- Shanghai Museum
- Renmin Park
- Grand Theatre
- Shanghai Art Museum

TIP

- For long, long views over the city, take the elevator to the lobby of the J.W. Marriott Hotel, in dazzling Tomorrow Square, or slowly revolve while dining within Epicure on 45, at the summit of the Radisson Hotel Shanghai New World.

If Shanghai's magnificent sprawl has a focal point, this is it. Many of the city's top attractions cluster here, among the swell of museum-goers, shoppers, white-collar workers and out-of-towners.

Bustling hub Redesigned in the 1990s, People's Square—perhaps the most popular name for city squares in China—is the equivalent of Beijing's Tiananmen Square, but is far more accessible. As Shanghai's largest Metro interchange, the square and its environs are constantly flooded with people, crossing over to Nanjing Donglu, doing exercises, flying kites or taking a break.

Seeing the sights The best way to negotiate People's Square (Renmin Guangchang) is to take the Metro exit to Renmin Dadao (People's

Clockwise from left: A small child feeds the pigeons; early-morning workers cross the square; outdoor exercises; kite-flying is a popular pastime; the top floors of the Radisson Hotel Shanghai New World, north of the square

Avenue), which divides the square in half. All places of interest, with the exception of the standout Shanghai Museum (▷ 42), are on the north side. Following the avenue east to west takes you past the Urban Planning Exhibition Hall (▷ 37) to the Grand Theatre (▷ 45), north of which is the distinctive clock tower of the Shanghai Art Museum (▷ 41), beyond which is the entrance to Renmin Park (▷ 40). Overlooking the square are some astronomically tall buildings, including Tomorrow Square, Brilliance Shimao International Plaza and the Radisson Hotel Shanghai New World (▷ 111). Unlike Beijing's Tiananmen Square, People's Square is not Stalinist in inspiration or surrounded by plain-clothes police. The square very much belongs to the people, who fill it with their own hobbies and pastimes, from ballroom dancing to pigeon-feeding and people-watching.

THE BASICS

- G6
- People's Square
- Restaurants and cafés
- People's Square
- 46, 71, 123, 574
- Good

Renmin Park

Enjoy the flowers in Renmin Park, especially the lotuses (right) in summer

THE BASICS

- G5–6
- Nanjing Xilu
- Daily 6–6
- People's Square
- 46, 71, 123, 574
- Inexpensive

HIGHLIGHTS

- Museum of Contemporary Art
- People-watching
- Unhurried park tempo
- Lotus flowers in summer

TIP

- Greet the dawn in the park with enthusiasts who rise early for a tai chi lesson.

People's Park (Renmin Gongyuan) evolved from a former British racecourse. A much-needed enclave of greenery and tranquillity, the park is an escape from the crowds of People's Square.

Park life Many visitors overlook the park, but it is lovely to have a stroll among its flower beds and manicured lawns. Be sure to visit the Museum of Contemporary Art (▷ 45), perhaps the chief attraction. Alongside the pond is Barbarossa (▷ 50), a popular Moroccan-style terrace bar and restaurant. The park attracts office workers at lunchtime and in summer any tree-shaded bench is much in demand. Summer is also the season to catch the gorgeous pink lotuses that flower in the waters of the main pond.

Gentle pursuits The racecourse had existed from 1862 and drew gamblers from around China, but it did not long survive the Communist takeover in 1949. Today, you'll see tai chi practitioners, stylized sword-fighters and kite flyers in the park's open spaces and on the adjoining People's Square (▷ 38). Groups of retired Chinese play mahjongg and chess, brush up on their ballroom dancing and English (native speakers out for a stroll are popular "victims" for the latter), and engage in match-making for their grandchildren, who are far too busy climbing the corporate ladder and having fun to find time for mere matrimony. Other parts of the park have narrow paths and fairly dense assemblages of trees and plants organized into a rigorously formal, landscaped setting.

Clock tower (left) and sculptures (right) outside the museum

Shanghai Art Museum

It's the architecture and lovely exhibition space within that steal the show of the British-built former racecourse club. This is one of Shanghai's gems, and that's before you even get to the art.

A bonus The building, dating from 1933, is worth seeing in its own right for its graceful clock tower, and because many original art deco features have survived. These include the horse's-head motifs on the balustrades, the original marble floors and wooden panels, and even a brick fireplace or two.

Exhibitions On the museum's five floors are 12 exhibition rooms, which cover Chinese paintings, ink-wash sketches, calligraphy and craft movements and periods from ancient to modern times. It's not only Chinese art that is accorded respect: Both classic and cutting-edge visiting international art exhibitions have already become something of a tradition (one exhibition was devoted to the fashion of Giorgio Armani).

The collection The museum's collection of modern Chinese art ranges from oil paintings and pop art to calligraphy and traditional Chinese painting. Frustratingly, there is little in the way of English translation, so the best times to visit are during the Shanghai Biennale or when the museum hosts exhibitions by both Chinese and international artists. Visitors can sign up for classes in traditional Chinese painting and sketching; and there are lectures, most, but not all, of which are in Chinese.

THE BASICS

www.sh-artmuseum.org.cn (in Chinese only)
G6
325 Nanjing Xilu
6327 2829
Daily 9–5; Biennale Oct–Nov, even years
Kathleen's 5 (▷ 51)
People's Square
46, 71, 123, 574
Few
Inexpensive

HIGHLIGHTS

- Clock tower of the old racecourse grandstand
- Temporary and visiting exhibitions
- Exhibitions at the Shanghai Biennale
- Kathleen's 5 restaurant (▷ 51), on the 5th floor

Shanghai Museum

HIGHLIGHTS

- Paintings and ceramics
- Bronzes and sculpture
- Excellent presentation

TIP

- The audio tour is a very good investment, guiding you through the museum's many highlights.

The Shanghai Museum contains China's foremost collection of ceramics, bronzes, art, calligraphy and Buddhist statues. You'll need a whole day to do it justice, and you could easily find yourself coming back for more.

The museum The museum's exterior is an eye-catching design, with its square base and circular crown, from which emanate four archlike handles—the ensemble is supposed to represent a Han dynasty bronze mirror or an ancient bronze *ding* tripod (an ancient food vessel). Built in the very heart of the city in 1996 to house a collection of some 120,000 cultural relics, the museum has 11 galleries and three exhibition halls. Despite tough competition, it quite possibly still ranks as the nation's best museum.

Clockwise from left: The imposing entrance to the museum; Yi water vessel from 771BC; stone lions guarding the courtyard; Qing dynasty (17th–20th century) woman's embroidered velvet jacket; a wider view showing the circular upper level; a painting of a woman with a sword

Exhibits The thematic layout and good lighting display the exhibits to their best advantage. The principal galleries—which you really should not miss—are dedicated to ceramics, ancient bronzes, ancient Chinese sculpture and paintings. The ceramics section in particular is stunning—a majestic sweep from early pottery fragments to the gorgeous imperial pieces of the Ming and Qing dynasties. The dark patina bronzes are similarly spectacular, displaying the elaborate animistic patterns and designs of pre-Buddhist China. The ancient Chinese sculpture pieces are largely Buddhist in inspiration and subject, forming what is possibly the best collection in China. Other galleries are devoted to ancient Chinese jade, Ming and Qing furniture, art from China's ethnic minorities and Chinese calligraphy. Don't miss the excellent museum shop (▷ 49).

THE BASICS

www.shanghaimuseum.net
- G6
- 201 Renmin Dadao
- 6372 3500
- Daily 9–5
- Cafés on the premises
- People's Square
- Few
- Free
- Audio tours

Xintiandi

Shikumen Open House Museum (left); a side street in the area (right)

THE BASICS

G7
Huangpi Nanlu
6311 2288
Many options
Huangpi Road (S)
13, 42, 63, 109
Good
Opposite Shikumen Museum Daily 10–10

HIGHLIGHTS

- *Shikumen* (stone-frame) houses
- Taipingqiao Park
- Trendy restaurants and cafés
- Boutique stores

TIP

- Xintiandi is just the first part of a redevelopment project of the zone around Taipingqiao Park. It is interesting to peruse the district to see how the changes are progressing. Be sure to take time out for a stroll around the handsome park, which has a pond at its heart.

A heavily restored and rebuilt quadrant of *shikumen* architecture, Xintiandi is a stylish blend of trendy bars and cafés, celebrated restaurants, boutiques, galleries, museums and clubs.

Housing project Shanghai's distinctive *shikumen* housing developed in the 19th century, a charming fusion of Chinese courtyard architecture and British terrace housing. By the early 1900s styles had changed and the houses started falling into disrepair. In the 1990s developers hit on the idea of preserving the architecture of one run-down 1930s *shikumen* area by changing the buildings' function from residential to shops and restaurants—while preserving the antique exteriors' walls and tiles.

Private history The history of the area and the cultural significance of the buildings are explained in the superb Shikumen Open House Museum (north block, Xintiandi; Sun–Thu 10.30am–11pm, Fri, Sat 11–11), which also presents a picture of the daily life of a typical family living here in the 1930s. The rooms are crammed with everyday objects and personal effects—movie posters, typewriters, radios, scent bottles, toys. The *tingzijian,* or "staircase room," between the first and second floors was usually rented out because its north-facing aspect made it cold in winter and stiflingly hot in summer. The pithily named Memorial House of the First National Congress of the Communist Party of China speaks for itself. The main exhibit is a waxwork diorama dramatizing the founding congress of the Chinese Communist Party.

More to See

GRAND THEATRE

China's first purpose-built opera house was designed by French architect Jean-Marie Charpentier and opened in 1998. Performances include opera, classical music and musicals. The main stage is vast.

G6 300 Renmin Dadao 6386 6666 People's Square

JING'AN SI (JING'AN TEMPLE)

The western part of Nanjing Lu was known as Bubbling Well Road until 1949. Before that it was Jing'an Road, named after this temple (the Temple of Tranquillity), which has stood here for over 1,700 years. The current buildings are largely rebuilt from earlier structures and the temple remains in a state of incomplete and fitful restoration.

C5 1686 Nanjing Xilu Daily Jing'an Temple 20, 37 None Inexpensive

SHANGHAI CENTRE

The colossal Shanghai Centre remains an expat fixture on Nanjing Lu, with bars, restaurants, a supermarket, Starbucks, the Shanghai Centre Theatre (▷ 50) and the still outstanding Portman Ritz-Carlton Shanghai hotel.

D5 1376 Nanjing Xilu 6279 8600 Jing'an Temple

SHANGHAI *LILONG* ARCHITECTURE

For some fantastic examples of Shanghai's *lilong* (alleyway) architecture, stroll west for around half a mile (around 1km) along Yuyuan Lu from the art deco Paramount Ballroom toward Zhenning Lu. On the way you'll pass some wonderfully preserved 1930s *lilong* alleys, complete with their characteristic houses.

C5

SHANGHAI MUSEUM OF CONTEMPORARY ART (MOCA)

A great addition to Shanghai's gallery selection, MOCA stages international exhibitions within a glass-walled and thoroughly modern exhibiting space.

G6 Renmin Park 6327 9900 Daily 9–5 People's Square Inexpensive

The Shanghai Acrobatic Troupe performs at the Shanghai Centre Theatre

Jing'an Si occupies a site used for temples for the last 1,700 years

蔡同德堂

Nanjing Lu and People's Square

Nanjing Lu may no longer be the only shopping street in Shanghai, but it remains Shanghai's—and perhaps China's—most famous road.

DISTANCE: 3km (2 miles) **ALLOW:** 1.5 hours (not including stops)

START

PEACE HOTEL (▷ 62)
J5 Nanjing Road (E)

❶ Rising up alongside this first section of Nanjing Donglu, from the Peace Hotel, is the occasional art deco building and, of course, plenty of shops.

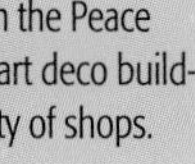

❷ Walk westward from the Nanjing Road (E) Metro station at Henan Zhonglu along the street's most famous section, the pedestrians-only stretch to People's Square (but watch out for traffic at the intersections).

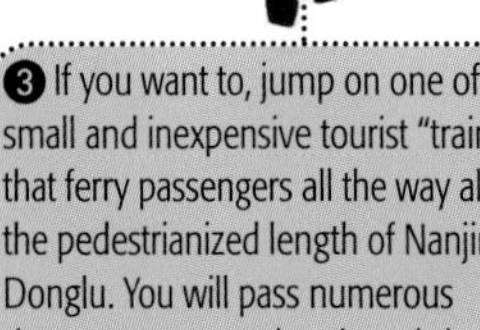

❸ If you want to, jump on one of the small and inexpensive tourist "trains" that ferry passengers all the way along the pedestrianized length of Nanjing Donglu. You will pass numerous department stores, hotels and shops, including the Duoyunxuan Art Studio at No. 422 (▷ 48).

❹ Pop into the Shanghai No. 1 Food Store (▷ 49), at No. 720, for every kind of Chinese snack.

❺ Cross Xizang Zhonglu to Nanjing Xilu and turn south into Renmin Park to visit the Shanghai Museum of Contemporary Art (▷ 45).

❻ Exit the park and walk west to the Shanghai Art Museum (▷ 41) or take the elevator to the foyer of the J.W. Marriott, high up in stunning Tomorrow Square. Walk south to the Grand Theatre (▷ 45), then east to the Urban Planning Exhibition Hall (▷ 37).

❼ Cross Renmin Dadao to the Shanghai Museum (▷ 42–43), the city's premier museum.

END

PEOPLE'S SQUARE (▷ 38–39)
G6 People's Square

Shopping

50 MOGANSHAN ROAD ART DISTRICT
Near Suzhou Creek in north Shanghai, this splendid concentration of contemporary art galleries, shops and cafés can easily take care of half a day. Look out for standout art galleries ShanghArt (www.shanghartgallery.com) and Art Scene Warehouse.
Off map ✉ 50 Moganshan Road ⏲ Hours vary, but most galleries open 10–6; some close Mon Ⓜ Shanghai Railway Station

CHATERHOUSE
If you're short of reading material while in Shanghai, pop into this well-stocked bookstore and browse its excellent range of fiction and non-fiction titles.
G7 ✉ Shop B-1E, Times Square, 93 Huaihai Donglu ☎ 6391 8237 ⏲ Daily 10–10 Ⓜ Huangpi Road (S)

CITY SHOP
www.cityshop.com.cn
Expats and visitors in town who have perhaps had one Chinese meal too many or are feeling the need for some familiar comfort food flock to the two branches of this sophisticated supermarket for international delicatessen items, familiar brand-name foodstuffs and more.
D5 ✉ Shanghai Centre, 1376 Nanjing Xilu ☎ 6215 0418 ⏲ Daily 8am–10pm Ⓜ Jing'an Temple

CYBERMART
Shanghai celebrates its fascination with things that bleep at this market leader in consumer electronics, which is packed with the latest, the finest and even occasionally the cheapest in everything from USB memory sticks to computers and DVD players.
G7 ✉ 282 Huaihai Zhonglu ☎ 6390 8008 ⏲ Daily 10–8 Ⓜ Huangpi Road (S)

DUOYUNXUAN ART STUDIO
Come here for calligraphy, paintings, stationery, rubbings of ancient carvings and seals.
H5 ✉ 422 Nanjing Donglu ☎ 6360 6475 ⏲ Daily 9.30–9.30 Ⓜ Nanjing Road (E)

HUA LIAN
This store was the renowned Wing On Department Store, and in its day, before the war, the latest thing in shopping. It has now been reborn as an international-style shopping center.
H5 ✉ 635 Nanjing Donglu ☎ 6322 4466 Ⓜ Nanjing Road (E) 🚌 20, 37

CLOISONNÉ

Bronze ornaments are covered in a network of copper strips and then filled with layers of enamel paint, before being fired and polished—this is cloisonné. Good pieces are hard to find, and the best tend to be found among the antiques.

ISETAN
Tokyo-based department store selling all the world's latest wares, though concentrating on items from Japan.
F7 ✉ 527 Huaihai Zhonglu ☎ 5306 1111 Ⓜ Shanxi Road (S) 🚌 26, 42, 911

LEI YUNG SHANG
Traditional Chinese medicines may look quaint in the slick setting of Nanjing Lu, but this venerable practitioner has plenty of customers.
F5 ✉ 719 Nanjing Xilu ☎ 6255 2708 ⏲ Daily 8.30am–9pm Ⓜ Nanjing Road (W)

NEW WORLD
From Adidas to Ermenegildo Zegna, by way of Cerruti 1881, Esprit, Lacoste, Swarovski and Versace, to name but a bare-bones few, the New World is nothing if not focused on known international brand names, and fits them all handily into its extensive floor space.
G5 ✉ 2–68 Nanjing Xilu ☎ 6358 8888 ⏲ Daily 10–10 Ⓜ People's Square

PLAZA 66
Arguably the pick of the malls lining Shanghai's main shopping street, Plaza 66 is the place to

head if money is no object. More than 100 designer brands are here, from Hermès to Bang & Olufsen.
E5 1266 Nanjing Xilu 6279 0910 Daily 10–10 Nanjing Road (W)

RAFFLES CITY
This Singaporean-owned mall has won plaudits for being a well-designed and comfortable place to shop. It's especially good for casual clothes, with a good spread of popular chains. There's also a cinema and spa.
G6 Xizang Zhonglu 6340 3600 Daily 10–10 People's Square

SHANGHAI FASHION COMPANY
Despite the name, this shop can't really compete in the fashion stakes with the newest shops selling chic international styles, but it does have an extensive range of clothes at moderate prices. It is in part of a venerable building that once housed one of Shanghai's original department stores.
H5 660–690 Nanjing Donglu 6352 5445 Daily 9.30am–10pm Nanjing Road (E)

SHANGHAI FOREIGN LANGUAGE BOOKSTORE
This place has a decent selection of books in English and other languages, and books covering China, its culture and language. It also sells CDs and stationery.
H6 390 Fuzhou Lu 6322 3200 Daily 9–7 Nanjing Road (E) 17, 49

SHANGHAI JINGDEZHEN PORCELAIN ARTWARE STORE
Porcelain and handicrafts, many of them from the kilns at Jingdezhen, in Jiangxi province.
E5 1175 Nanjing Xilu 6253 0885 Daily 10–10 Nanjing Road (W) 20, 37

SHANGHAI MUSEUM SHOP
In fact, there are three shops on the southern side of the museum, which specialize in books, antiques and antique reproductions.
G6 201 Renmin Dadao 6372 3500 Daily 9–5 People's Square 23

SHANGHAI NO. 1 FOOD STORE
This large supermarket stocks mainly Chinese products but has a growing range of international brands. It is a good resource for putting together a picnic or for stocking up for days when you don't want to eat out at a restaurant.
H5 720 Nanjing Donglu 6322 2777 Daily 9.30am–10pm Nanjing Road (E) 20, 37

CLOTHES

Probably the best place for clothes shopping is Huaihai Zhonglu, the main road of the French Concession district, where several shops specialize in designer clothes imported from Hong Kong, and other designer shops have appeared in the last few years.

WELLCOME SUPERMARKET
This is an expensive Hong Kong supermarket selling Western and Japanese produce.
D5 1376 Nanjing Xilu 6279 8018 Jing'an Temple 37

WESTGATE MALL
Another of the shopping malls that have sprouted along Nanjing Lu. Its stores feature haute couture, street-cred fashion boutiques and other requisites of an upwardly aspiring lifestyle.
E5 1038 Nanjing Xilu 6218 7878 Daily 10–10 Nanjing Road (W)

ZHANG'S TEXTILES
One of the few places where you are sure to find a genuine antique, Zhang's sells fabulous embroideries from the Qing dynasty. (For regulations on exporting antiques, ▷ 78, panel.)
D5 Room 202a, Shanghai Centre, 1376 Nanjing Xilu 6279 8587 Daily 10–9.30 Jing'an Temple

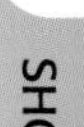

Entertainment and Nightlife

BARBAROSSA
This Moroccan-themed bar, next to the pond in Renmin Park, is ideal for unwinding to great music.
G5 Renmin Park, 231 Nanjing Xilu 6318 0220 Daily 11am–2am People's Square

BIG BAMBOO
Perhaps the ultimate Shanghai sports bar, Big Bamboo has an unrepentant dedication to beer, Western food, pool and back-to-back sports viewing.
D5 132 Nanyang Lu 6256 2265 Daily 11am–2am Jing'an Temple

GRAND THEATRE
See page 45.

JING'AN HOTEL
Offering quite a step up from the usual piano player or small music combo in the lobby, the Jing'an Hotel lobby is the venue for weekly chamber music concerts by musicians from the highly regarded Shanghai Symphony Orchestra.
C6 370 Huashan Lu 6248 1888, ext. 617 Jing'an Temple

LONG BAR
Popular with expats, this venue is named after Shanghai's famous bar in the now defunct Shanghai Club.
D5 2nd floor, Shanghai Centre, 1376 Nanjing Xilu 6279 8268 Daily 10am–2am Jing'an Temple

MAJESTIC THEATRE
Traditional Chinese opera, music and dance are performed at one of the city's finest old theaters.
E5 66 Jiangning Lu 6217 4409 Nanjing Road (W)

MALONE'S BAR
This American-style bar offers a good range of bar food, live music and heavy doses of sports TV.
D5 257 Tongren Lu Daily 10am–2am Jing'an Temple

SHANGHAI CENTRE THEATRE
One of the highlights of the multiuse Shanghai Centre (▷ 45), the theater puts on Chinese and international music, opera, drama and dance, along with performances by the stellar Shanghai Acrobatic Theatre.
D5 Shanghai Centre, 1376 Nanjing Xilu 6279 8948 Jing'an Temple

CHINESE OPERA

Chinese opera is completely unlike Western opera. Foreigners find it difficult to appreciate at first, but it is worth trying at least once. The singing style is falsetto and the action heavily stylized, but overall it is very colorful and can be highly dramatic, especially if battles are staged using acrobatic techniques. Check the local press for performances.

SHANGHAI CONCERT HALL
This handsome venue was built as the Nanking Theatre in 1930. It was moved, brick by brick, 216ft (66m) to its present site in 2004. The 1,200-seat concert hall hosts the Shanghai Symphony Orchestra and visiting artists.
G6 523 Yan'an Donglu 6386 2836 People's Square 46, 71, 123, 574

SKY DOME BAR
Crowning the Radisson Hotel, this is one of the top places to come for truly astral views of Shanghai that put extra fizz in your gin and tonic.
G5 47th floor, Radisson Hotel Shanghai New World, 88 Nanjing Xilu 6359 9999 Daily 5pm–1am People's Square

STUDIO CITY
A six-screen multiplex at the top of a modern shopping mall. The films are Chinese and international, with some shown in their original English.
E5 10th Floor, Westgate Mall, 1038 Nanjing Xilu 6218 2173 Nanjing Road (W)

TIANCHAN YIFU THEATRE
Head to this theater, which was renovated in 2004, for Chinese opera.
G–H6 701 Fuzhou Lu 6351 4668; reservations 6217 2426 People's Square 46, 71, 123, 574

Restaurants

PRICES

Prices are approximate, based on a 3-course meal for one person.
$$$ more than 250RMB
$$ 100–250RMB
$ under 100RMB

BELLA NAPOLI ($)

This good-value restaurant serves excellent pasta and other Italian dishes in an enjoyable setting.
D5 140 Xikang Lu 6253 8358 Daily 11.30–2, 6–11 Nanjing Road (W)

BRASIL STEAKHOUSE ($)

Waiters revolve around tables with hefty skewers of all-you-can-eat grilled meat at this popular restaurant—best if you're in a group.
C6 1649 Nanjing Xilu 6255 9898 Daily 11–3, 5–11 Jing'an Temple

ELEMENT FRESH ($)

Long hours and healthy international food (sandwiches, salads, juices) are on the menu at this ever-popular café with several branches in Shangahi.
D5 Room 112, Shanghai Centre, 1376 Nanjing Xilu 6279 8682 Daily 7am–11pm Jing'an Temple

FU LIN XUAN ($$–$$$)

The glass-and-wood decor is stylish and the Cantonese seafood is pretty good, though service can be variable.
E7 37 Sinan Lu 6372 1777 Daily lunch, dinner Huangpi Road (S) 24

GONGDELIN ($–$$)

A famous vegetarian restaurant where the dishes are imitations of meat (using tofu).
F6 445 Nanjing Xilu 6327 0218 Daily lunch, dinner People's Square 20, 27

KATHLEEN'S 5 ($$–$$$)

On the fifth floor of the Shanghai Art Museum (and with a glassed-in rooftop terrace), this smart restaurant serves American-based cuisine that roams the world for elements to mix and match, with local influences. Brunch is served from 11am on weekends.
G6 325 Nanjing Xilu 6327 2221 Mon–Thu 11.30am–midnight, Fri 11.30am–1am, Sat, Sun 11am–1am People's Square 46, 71, 123, 574

SOUP

In the West it is customary to have soup as a starter or appetizer, but in China soup is generally served toward the end of the meal as a sort of "digestif," and on informal occasions is also a way of helping to finish remains in the rice bowl. At formal functions such as banquets, soup is served in a separate bowl.

LYNN ($–$$)

Excellent, modern and eye-catching Shanghai cuisine in a sharp and stylish environment. Try the crispy duck or the deep-fried spare ribs.
D5 99-1 Xikang Lu 6247 0101 Daily 11.30–10.30 Nanjing Road (W)

MEI LONG ZHEN ($$)

In the former Communist Party headquarters, this restaurant serves food in Huaiyang, Sichuan and Shanghainese styles. Deep-fried *gui* (fish), tofu dishes and cold shredded jellyfish are on the menu.
G6 1081 Nanjing Xilu 6253 5353 Daily lunch, dinner Nanjing Road (W) 37

T8 ($$–$$$)

At the heart of Xintiandi, elegant T8 is one of Shanghai's very best restaurants for international dishes and pure ambience. Treat yourself.
G7 No. 8, North Block Xintiandi, Lane 181 Taicang Lu 6355 8999 Daily 11.30–2.30, 6.30–11.30 Huangpi Road (S)

VEGETARIAN LIFESTYLE ($–$$)

Excellent meat-free, organic and MSG-devoid Chinese food—all tasty and imaginatively created. The restaurant has plenty of returning customers and two other branches.
E5 258 Fengxian Lu 6215 7566 Daily 10–9 Nanjing Road (W)

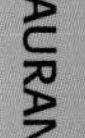

The Bund/Waitan

Stretching north from Renmin Lu on the edge of the Old City to Suzhou Creek, the Bund is Shanghai's premier promenade. From here you have a stunning view across the water to Pudong's glittering towers.

3
4
5
6
7
Tiantong
Lu
Shanxi Beilu
Beilu
Qipu Lu
Jiangxi
Beilu
Fujian
Shanxi
Beilu
HENAN
BEILU
SICHUAN
BEILU
Tanggu
Wuchang
Lu
Zhapu
Lu
Tiantong
Lu
Shanghai
Post Museum
Suzhou
Beilu
Suzhou
Creek
Suzhou
Beilu
Suzhou
Nanlu
Suzhou
Nanlu
Hong
Kong
Lu
Lu
Lu
SICHUAN ZHONGLU
Zhonglu
Huqiu
mingyuan
WAIBAIDU
BRIDGE
BEIJING
DONGLU
Monument to the
People's Heroes
Huangpu
Park
Jiangxi
Yuan-
Bank of
China
Dianchi Lu
NANJING DONGLU
Peace
Hotel
Chen Yi
Monument
Jiujiang
Lu
Bund
Sightseeing
Tunnel
Hankou
Lu
Zhonglu
HENAN
ZHONGLU
Zhonglu
Sichuan Zhonglu
ZHONGSHAN DONG 1-LU
The Bund
Fuzhou Lu
Fujian Zhonglu
Shandong
Guangdong
Lu
Studio
Rouge
Guangdong
Lu
Shanghai
Gallery of Art
Wuhu Lu
Jiangxi
YAN'AN
DONGLU
YAN'AN DONGLU TUNNEL
Ninghai
Donglu
Fujian Nanlu
0
400 m
0
400 yds
H
J

WUSONG LU
Hanyang Lu
Xi'an Lu
Hongkou
Nanxun Lu
Liyang
Tanggu Lu
Emei Lu
Minhang
Dongchangzhi Lu
Lushun Lu
Liling Lu
Shanggiu
Yongding Lu
Changzhi Lu
Tanggu Lu
Branch
Machang Lu
Lu
DAMING LU
DONGDAMING LU
Astor House Hotel
Minhang Lu
Nanxun Lu
Huangpu Lu
International Passenger Terminal
Huangpu
K
L

Around Suzhou Creek

HIGHLIGHTS

- Waibaidu Bridge
- Former British Consulate
- Russian Consulate
- Astor House Hotel
- Broadway Mansions
- Shanghai Post Museum

TIP

- It is more pleasant these days to stroll the riverside paths along either bank. The occasional sorry-looking green scraps of yore have been joined by riverside parks, gardens and walkways, with more to follow in the years to come.

Long a feature of the Shanghai landscape, Suzhou Creek came to represent much that was unattractive in Shanghai's rush to develop. Today, it's a sign of how the city is cleaning up its act.

The colonial period Suzhou Creek separated the British and American Concession, and the creek banks close to the Huangpu River have some architectural survivors from this time. The Broadway Mansions Hotel, at 20 Suzhou Beilu, is in an art deco masterpiece that was the Shanghai Mansions (1934). Also on the north bank, the Astor House Hotel (▷ 63), at 15 Huangpu Lu, is a historic survivor from concession days, as is the Russian Consulate opposite. The twin-span steel Waibaidu (Garden) Bridge, which crosses over the creek alongside Huangpu Park (▷ 63), dates from 1907,

Clockwise from left: Vessels line the sides of the creek and traffic passes along the middle; selling bicycle registrations near Suzhou Bridge; the Russian Consulate building; a new apartment block on the creekside; Suzhou Creek artists' quarter

replacing a wooden bridge; it was taken away for restoration in 2008 and put back in 2009. The old Shanghai Post Office building, at 276 Suzhou Beilu, houses the intriguing Shanghai Post Museum.

Troubled waters From its source in Tai Hu (Lake Tai) close to Suzhou, the creek flows east through some of China's most polluted territory before debouching into the Huangpu River at the north end of the Bund. By 1998, when the first clean-up measures were introduced, Suzhou Creek's once crystal-clear water had become a black open sewer. Those who lived beside the creek—a fate reserved for the poor—could not open their windows in summer so bad was the smell. The Suzhou Creek Rehabilitation Project has changed things for the better. More needs to be done, but fish are returning.

THE BASICS

West and north from K5

Suzhou Nanlu and Suzhou Beilu

Nanjing Road (E)

20, 42, 55, 65

The Bund

HIGHLIGHTS

- Panoramic views
- Waterfront European-style buildings
- Boat trips on the Huangpu River (▷ 60)

TIP

- The Bund shows different faces of itself during the day: Early morning tai chi practitioners give way to rush-hour crowds, then a period of calm before the lunchtime and afternoon strollers emerge. Evening, the time for leisure crowds, is followed by those out to view the lights.

Arriving by ship from Europe or America in the 1930s, the expatriate's first view of Shanghai would have been the waterfront street known as the Bund, a grand slice of the colonial world that is still impressive today.

Waitan The Bund (a word of Anglo-Indian origin meaning "waterfront" or "embankment") is now known as Waitan or Zhongshan Dong Yilu (or 1-Lu). It runs along the Huangpu River from Suzhou Creek in the north to Yan'an Lu in the south. The buildings lining it date from the early 20th century and are largely Western in style. The Bund is where modern Shanghai began and it remains the city's grandest display. A "must do" activity is to stroll the Bund after dark, when the illuminated waterfront and the view to Pudong create a memorable view.

Clockwise from left: A flag flying atop the Customs House clock tower; statue of Chen Yi, the first mayor of Shanghai; the Bund viewed from the Riverside Promenade; tai chi exercises; a bronze lion outside the Hong Kong and Shanghai Bank

The buildings Although changes have been made—the trams have gone, as have the old "go-downs," or warehouses, and statues of foreigners—the Bund would be instantly recognizable to a 1930s resident. A walk from south to north would begin with the Shanghai Club at No. 3, which claimed to have the longest bar in the world. The domed building at No. 12 was the Hong Kong and Shanghai Bank, built in 1921; it is definitely worth popping in to look at the beautiful ceiling mosaics inside. Next door, surmounted by a clock once known as Big Ching, is the Customs House of 1927. Next to the main building of the Peace Hotel (▷ 62) on the corner of Nanjing Lu (Nanking Road) is the Bank of China (1937). No. 27 was the headquarters of Jardine Matheson, one of the early companies to prosper from the opium trade, and No. 33 was the old British Consulate.

THE BASICS

- J6–K5
- Zhongshan Dong 1-Lu
- Various restaurants and cafés
- Nanjing Road (E)
- None

Huangpu Riverboat Tour

HIGHLIGHTS

- Fabulous panoramas of both the Bund and Lujiazui in Pudong
- Confluence with the mighty Yangtze River
- Yangpu Bridge

TIP

- Should a cruise on the Huangpu take up more time or money than you can afford, try instead the cross-river ferries, which you can think of as giving a cheap microcruise on the river.

The Huangpu and Yangtze rivers are the original reasons for Shanghai's prosperity. A river cruise along the Huangpu will show aspects of this huge city you might not otherwise see.

Two rivers The Yangtze is the longest river in China. Rising in the Tibetan Plateau, it meanders right across the country, passing through several provinces, and, most famously, the Three Gorges. The Huangpu, only 68 miles (110km) in length, runs from Lake Tai and empties into the Yangtze River some 17 miles (28km) downstream. Its average width through the city is 1,300ft (400m) and its average depth 26ft (8m). Large ships were able to enter the wide mouth of the Yangtze, make the short journey up the Huangpu and unload their cargoes at the wharves along the

Clockwise from left: A plaque showing the level of the Huangpu flood in 1997; looking across the river from the Bund to Pudong; a night-time view across to Pudong with the Oriental Pearl Tower prominent to the left of center

Bund. The goods were transported by barges along Suzhou Creek and then along the network of canals for distribution throughout China.

Touring the Huangpu Boat tours leave from the south section of the Bund, south of the intersection with Yan'an Donglu. The shortest trips merely journey to Yangpu Bridge or other bridges crossing the Huangpu River, while the longest trip is the three-and-a-half-hour return journey to Wusongkou at the mouth of the Yangtze River. If you travel first class, the trip to Wusongkou and back is comfortable. You first pass Suzhou Creek, then the architecture of the brand new Shanghai Port International Ferry Terminal and Yangpu Bridge. You will also pass Fuxing Island, where Chiang Kai Shek made his last stand before fleeing to Taiwan. Finally, you meet the Yangtze, before returning to the Bund.

THE BASICS

- L5
- Boats leave from the south section of the Bund, south of the intersection with Yan'an Donglu (J6)
- 6374 4461
- Cruises depart daily every 2 hours or so 9am–10pm
- Bar on board ship
- 20, 42, 55, 65
- None
- Moderate–tickets through CITS or from a kiosk close to the pier
- Performances often given on river cruise

Peace Hotel

The Peace Hotel alongside the Bank of China (left); the hotel's Old Jazz Band (right)

THE BASICS

www.shanghaipeacehotel.com
J5
20 Nanjing Donglu
6321 6888
The hotel closed for renovations in 2007; it is due to reopen in 2010
Café, bar and restaurant on premises
Nanjing Road (E)
37, 42, 55, 65
None
Free, unless you spend the night

HIGHLIGHTS

- Art deco architecture
- Art deco details in the lobby

The Peace Hotel is the most iconic art deco building in Shanghai. During its heyday, this was *the* place to stay and the patina of its pyramid roof is one of the Bund's most distinctive images.

The Sassoons Of the many families of Sephardic Jews that flourished in prewar Shanghai, the most famous is the Sassoon family. Fleeing an intolerant Baghdad in the 18th century to make a fortune in Bombay, they then proceeded to buy warehouses in Shanghai. Successive generations invested in the port, but it was Victor Sassoon who built the well-known landmark on the Bund now known as the Peace Hotel. Though it represents the hated era of foreign domination, many new skyscrapers ape its distinctive pyramidical roof design.

The Cathay There had been a Sassoon House on the Bund for some time, but Victor Sassoon had visions of a skyscraper as a modern business headquarters and wanted to include a fabulous hotel into the bargain. Today's Peace Hotel, originally the Cathay, dates from 1930, with art deco ironwork and high ceilings inside and looking somewhat like a smaller Empire State Building outside. The lowest four floors were reserved for offices; the remainder were given over to what Victor hoped would be the finest hotel in the East. It had the best technology and service that the period could offer, while the Horse & Hounds Bar became the most fashionable rendezvous in the city. The Peace Hotel closed in 2007 for renovations and is due to reopen some time in 2010.

More to See

ASTOR HOUSE HOTEL

www.astorhousehotel.com

Now restored as a fancy hotel (▷ 110), this building just across the bridge at the northern end of the Bund, opposite the Russian Consulate, was once one of the city's finest hotels.

K5 15 Huangpu Lu 6324 6388 Daily Nanjing Road (E) 28 None Free

BUND SIGHTSEEING TUNNEL

This psychedelically lit tunnel runs under the water from the Bund, opposite Nanjing Donglu, to the Pudong shore. You board an unmanned miniature train car for the four-minute ride, during which a sound-and-light show unfolds, with images projected on the walls of the tunnel.

J6–K6 Zhongshan Dong 1-Lu (the Bund) Mon–Thu 8am–10.30pm, Fri–Sun 8am–11pm (to 10pm daily Nov–Mar) Nanjing Road (E) 65 Moderate

HUANGPU PARK

At the northern end of the Bund near the bridge, this is the infamous park where a notice was said to forbid entry to "Dogs and Chinese" (the wording was not exactly like that, in fact). It is a pleasant park with an ugly monument, beneath which is a small museum about old Shanghai.

K5 Zhongshan Dong 1-Lu (the Bund) Summer daily 6am–10pm; winter 6–6 Nanjing Road (E) None Free

SHANGHAI GALLERY OF ART

www.threeonthebund.com

This exclusive gallery, in the prestigious Three on the Bund shopping, dining and entertainment complex, displays contemporary art.

J6 3rd floor, Three on the Bund, Zhongshan Dong 1-Lu 6321 5757 See website for exhibition dates Free Nanjing Road (E)

STUDIO ROUGE

www.studiorouge.cn

Visit this minimalist gallery to see contemporary photography and art.

J6 17 Fuzhou Lu 6323 0833 Daily 10.30–6.30 Free Nanjing Road (E)

Early morning exercises in Huangpu Park

A street artist in Huangpu Park

The Bund

The very symbol of 19th-century foreign interventions in China, the Bund (▷ 58–59) was where the story of modern Shanghai began.

DISTANCE: 1.2 miles (2km) **ALLOW:** Up to 1 hour

START

SUZHOU CREEK (▷ 56)
K5 Nanjing Road (E)

❶ From Waibaidu Bridge at Suzhou Creek, walk south down the west side of Zhongshan Dong 1-Lu. One of the first buildings you will see is the former British Consulate, behind the gates at No. 33.

❷ Nos. 24–27 are early-20th-century buildings that house banks, as is the 1920s mini-skyscraper at No. 23, the Bank of China building.

❸ The Peace Hotel (▷ 62) stands at the intersection of Nanjing Donglu and Zhongshan Dong 1-Lu. Across Nanjing Donglu is a second wing of the Peace Hotel, in what was the Palace Hotel.

❹ Continue south, crossing Jiujiang Lu, Hankou Lu and Fuzhou Lu, taking in details on buildings like the Customs House at No. 13 and the former Hong Kong and Shanghai Bank at No. 12.

❺ On the south side of Guangdong Lu, at No. 3, is the stellar Three on the Bund shopping, dining and entertainment complex.

❻ Cross over Zhongshan Dong 1-Lu, and go north along the Bund's waterfront promenade, affording you a different view of the buildings you have just passed, and views of the river and Pudong.

❼ At the north end of the Bund, stroll through Huangpu Park (▷ 63), then cross Waibaidu Bridge to visit the venerable Astor House Hotel on the north side of Suzhou Creek.

ASTOR HOUSE HOTEL (▷ 63)
J5 Nanjing Road (E)

END

Shopping

BLUE SHANGHAI WHITE
Perfect hand-painted ceramic gifts—simple, but lovely.
J6 Room 103, 17 Fuzhou Lu 6352 2222 Daily 10.30–6.30pm Nanjing Road (E)

LAO ZHOU HU CHENG CHINESE WRITING BRUSH AND INKSTICK STORE
This shop supplies the items needed for traditional Chinese painting and calligraphy—brushes, inkstones and ink slabs, for example.
J5 90 Henan Zhonglu 6323 0924 Nanjing Road (E) 66

SILK KING
One of Shanghai's most popular silk outlets for silk by the meter or tailor-made clothes.
J5 588 Nanjing Donglu 6352 2398 Nanjing Road (E)

SUZHOU COBBLERS
www.suzhou-cobblers.com
Choose from a wide range of exquisite hand-embroidered Chinese silk slippers, or pick one of the handbags that come in a variety of hues and designs, for a special reminder of your time in Shanghai.
J6 Room 101, 17 Fuzhou Lu 6329 9656 Daily 10–6.30 Nanjing Road (E)

Entertainment and Nightlife

ATTICA
Up-to-the-minute Bund-side club with some spectacular nocturnal views from its rooftop terraces.
J7 11th floor, 15 Zhongshan Dong 2-Lu (the Bund) 6373 3588 Wed–Sat 9pm–late (bar 5pm–late) Nanjing Road (E)

BAR ROUGE
High up amid the setting of Bund 18 is the coolest cocktail bar in town, its atmosphere ramped up by name DJs after midnight and its night-time outlook a big draw by itself.
J6 18 Zhongshan Dong 1-Lu (the Bund) 6339 1199 Mon–Thu 3pm–2am, Fri, Sat 3pm–4am; special brunch Sat, Sun noon–4pm Nanjing Road (E) 37, 42, 55, 65

CAPTAIN'S BAR
Atop the Captain Hostel (▷ 109), this lively and inexpensive bar has an excellent terrace with mesmerizing views of Lujiazui.
J6 6th floor, Captain Hostel, 36 Fuzhou Lu 6323 7869 Daily 11am–2am Nanjing Road (E)

D & G MARTINI BAR
You'll find cocktails and a chic ambience for the fashionable set here.
J6 1st floor, 6 Zhongshan Dong 1-Lu (the Bund) 6339 1200 Daily 10.30am–late Nanjing Road (E)

GLAMOUR BAR
This gorgeous bar has much expanded by moving down from upstairs into a much larger space. The cocktails are fabulous, the views are vibrant and the ambience is stylish without being exclusively exclusive.
J6 6th Floor, 20 Guangdong Lu 6350 9988 Daily 5pm–2 or 3am Nanjing Road (E) 37, 42, 55, 65

Restaurants

PRICES

Prices are approximate, based on a 3-course meal for one person.

$$$ more than 250RMB
$$ 100–250RMB
$ under 100RMB

AJISEN ($)

Ajisen's scrumptious Japanese noodles have developed a loyal following across the entire land. Service is efficient, although you may have to wait for a table. The photo menu makes choosing your food easy; you pay at the start of the meal.

J5 327 Nanjing Donglu 6360 7194 Daily 10am–11pm Nanjing Road (E)

BUND 12 CAFÉ ($–$$)

A great opportunity to look inside one of the Bund's venerable landmark buildings. The café, on the second floor, is a miniature masterpiece of period refurbishment, with an original marble fireplace and art deco light fittings. A balcony with terrace tables overlooks the courtyard. The menu includes sandwiches, salads, pasta, pizzas, cakes and fresh fruit juices.

J6 Room 226, 12 Zhongshan Dong 1-Lu (the Bund) 6329 5896 Daily lunch, dinner Nanjing Road (E) 37, 42, 55, 65

FEST BREW HOUSE ($–$$)

A beerhall that sells the only home-brewed beer in Shanghai, as well as serving the dishes to go with it—baked fish, oxtail soup, or pork Lyonnaise.

J6 11 Hankou Lu 6321 8447 Daily 11–11 Nanjing Road (E) 49

JEAN GEORGES ($$–$$$)

Offering stupendous dishes in a lavish setting, this is one of Shanghai's best restaurants for modern Western cuisine.

J6 4th floor, Three on the Bund, 3 Zhongshan Dong 1-Lu 6321 7733 Daily 11am–1am Nanjing Road (E)

M ON THE BUND ($$)

M on the Bund serves European dishes and is one of Shanghai's best restaurants, especially if you can grab a terrace table with its wonderful views. Reserve ahead.

J6 7th floor, 20 Guangdong Lu 6350 9988 Daily 11.30–2.30, 6.15–10.30 Nanjing Road (E)

DUMPLINGS

Like north China's famous *jiaozi* (dumplings), Shanghai's signature dish—copied across the nation—is *xialongbao* (pronounced "seeyaolong-bough"). Small, steamed, plump dumplings, *xiaolong-bao* come in a variety of fillings, from pork to crab meat, arriving at the table in steamers. Bite carefully, as the meat juice is scalding.

NEW HEIGHTS ($)

Put yourself up there with the best: It's a tall order not to be won over by the Shanghai views at night at this bar-cum-restaurant, serving international cuisine.

J6 7th floor, Three on the Bund, 3 Zhongshan Dong 1-Lu 6321 0909 Daily noon–10.30pm Nanjing Road (E)

SENS & BUND ($$$)

This fabulous Bund-side European restaurant, from the Pourcel twins, offers a lavish and much-admired menu.

J6 6th floor, Bund 18, 18 Zhongshan Dong 1-Lu 6323 9898 Daily 11.30–2.30, 6.30–9.45 Nanjing Road (E)

WHAMPOA CLUB ($$$)

Run by one of Shanghai's celebrity chefs, Jereme Leung, this ineffably smart restaurant, on the fifth floor of the glitzy Three on the Bund center, offers a contemporary, fusion take on Shanghai cuisine to tasteful effect.

J6 Three on the Bund, 3 Zhongshan Dong 1-Lu (entrance at 17 Guangdong Lu) 6321 3737 Daily 11.30–2.30, 5.30–11 Nanjing Road (E) 37, 42, 55, 65

The rickety Old Town contains the Yu Garden, the Yuyuan Bazaar, Huxinting Tea House, several notable temples and antiques markets, and an escape from Shanghai's more frantic districts.

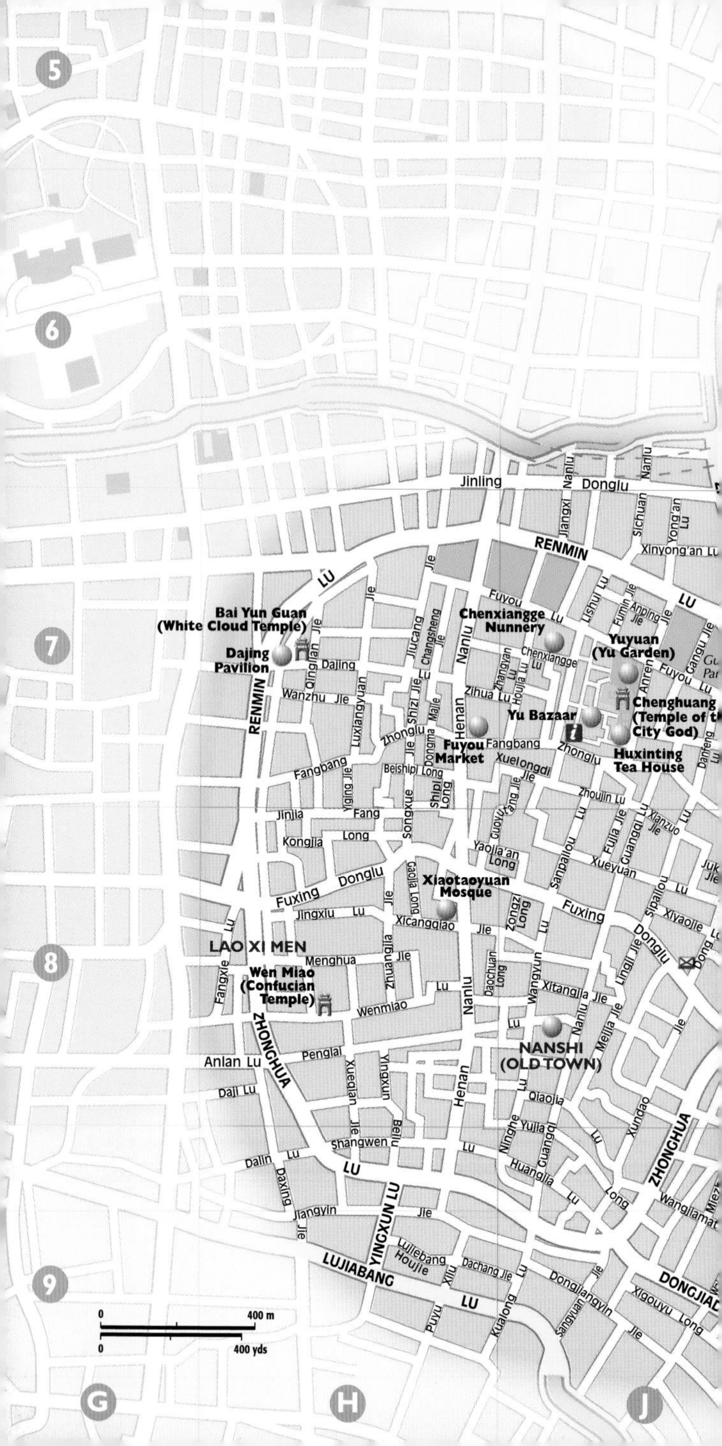

5
6
7
8
9
G
H
J
Jinling
Donglu
Nanlu
Jiangxi
Sichuan
Yong'an Lu
RENMIN
LU
Xinyong'an Lu
Bai Yun Guan (White Cloud Temple)
Dajing Pavilion
Qinglian Jie
Dajing
Wanzhu Jie
Jiucang
Changsheng Jie
Fuyou
Chenxiangge Nunnery
Chenxiangge Lu
Lishui Lu
Fumin Jie
Anping Jie
Yuyuan (Yu Garden)
Anren
Fuyou Lu
Gangu Jie
Chenghuang (Temple of the City God)
Yu Bazaar
Huxinting Tea House
Zihua Lu
Houjia Lu
Zhangyan Lu
Shizi Jie
Majie
Henan
Fuyou Market
Fangbang
Zhonglu
Luxiangyuan
Dongma Long
Beishipi Long
Shipi Long
Xuelongdi Jie
Yiqing Jie
Songxue
Jinjia Fang
Kongjia Long
Long
Guoyutang Jie
Zhoujin Lu
Xianzuo Jie
Fujia Jie
Guangqi Lu
Sanpailou Lu
Yaojia'an Long
Xueyuan
Fuxing Donglu
Jingxiu Lu
Jie
Gaojia Long
Xiaotaoyuan Mosque
Xicangqiao
Fuxing
Zongzi Long
Sipailou Lu
Xiyaojie
Donglu
LAO XI MEN
Fangxie Lu
Menghua Jie
Zhuangjia
Wen Miao (Confucian Temple)
Wenmiao Lu
Nanlu
Dachuan Long
Wangyun Lu
Xitangjia Jie
Nanlu
Meijia Jie
Lingji Jie
ZHONGHUA
NANSHI (OLD TOWN)
Anlan Lu
Penglai
Xueqian Jie
Yingxun
Beilu
Henan
Daji Lu
Qiaojia
Yujia
Guangqi
Ninghe Lu
Shangwen
Huangjia
Xundao
Dalin Lu
Daxing Jie
LU
Jiangyin Jie
YINGXUN LU
Lu
Long
Wangjiamatou
LUJIABANG
Lujiebang Houjie
Xilu
Dachang Jie
Donglijiangyin Jie
Sangyuan
Xigouyu Long
DONGJIADU
LU
Puyu
Kualong
0
400 m
0
400 yds

Old Town/Nanshi
Huangpu
FUXING DONGLU TUNNEL
ZHONGSHAN NANLU
Waima Lu
Long
Jie
Yangjiadu Hengjie
Laobaidu Hengjie
DONGLU
Baidu
Maojia
Doushi
Xinmatou
Lu
Huayi Jie
Long
Dongjiadu Cathedral
2-LU
TUNNEL
K
L

Huxinting Tea House

HIGHLIGHTS

- Charming building in entertaining location
- Cooling on hot days

TIP

- When the waiter or waitress refills your tea cup, tapping the index and second fingers of your right hand is a traditional way to indicate "thank you" for being served tea–the gesture represents the kowtow that everyone had to do in the presence of the emperor.

The delightful old tea house, in its watery setting in the middle of a lake, is the focal point of the Old Town. It fits in with the China of popular imagination, a China that has all but disappeared.

Tea drinking Tea is widely produced throughout central and southern China and is also widely consumed in everyday life–taxi drivers often keep a jar with them, half filled with leaves to which boiling water is added throughout the day; there will probably be tea in your hotel room; and when people meet, or at an official function, tea will certainly be served at some point. In the past, every town had several tea houses, where conversation was an adjunct to an appreciation of good teas. However, an appreciation of fine teas and the art of tea drinking in its ceremonial form,

Clockwise from top left: A suited waiter in the tea house; people negotiating the Nine Zig-Zag Bridge to the tea house; visitors to Shanghai enjoying tea; the tea house illuminated at night; relaxing with tea and snacks

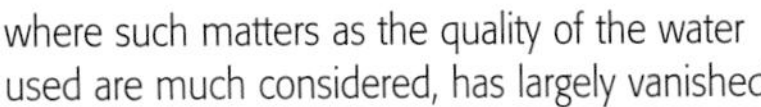

where such matters as the quality of the water used are much considered, has largely vanished.

Huxinting The Huxinting Tea House, surrounded by a small lake, is truly the hub of the Old Town. Its precise origins are not entirely clear, but it dates from some time during the Ming dynasty, was renovated as a brokerage house in 1784, and became a tea house in 1856. It was originally part of both the Temple of the City God (▷ 75) and Yuyuan (▷ 74). As Shanghai prospered, parts of the garden, including the tea house, were purchased by local merchants, who used it as a meeting place for conducting business. A building of great charm, it is approached via the Nine Zig-Zag Bridge, over waters glittering with goldfish. Inside you may drink good-quality tea from traditional teapots—refreshing on hot summer days.

THE BASICS

- J7
- 257 Yuyuan Lu
- 6373 6950
- Daily 8.30am–10pm
- Plenty of restaurants nearby, in the Old Town
- 11, 14, 26
- None
- Moderate
- Tea ceremony performed in the evening

Old Town

TOP 25

HIGHLIGHTS

- A hint of the atmosphere of old China
- Excellent snack food and shops

TIP

- Most visitors to the Old Town focus on its northern section, around Yuyuan and the Huxinting Tea House. But there's much more to the district than this, and, if anything, the other parts are more authentic.

One of the unexpected pleasures of Shanghai is to discover, amid the high-rise modernity, an old Chinese town—the original Shanghai. In its narrow streets you can absorb something of the atmosphere and bustle of traditional China.

History Until the Treaty of Nanking in 1842, Shanghai was a moderately important walled town concentrated in the area now called Nanshi. The walls were pulled down in 1912 to provide better access for shops and traders, but even now the area is self-contained and the route of the old walls can be traced along Renmin Lu and Zhonghua Lu. A single chunk of wall survives at the Dajing Pavilion (▷ 75). Some of Shanghai's most ancient temples survive in the Old Town, including the Wen Miao (Confucius Temple; ▷ 76), the Chenghuang

Clockwise from top left: Collectibles at Dongtai Lu antiques market; an Old Town tailor hard at work on her sewing machine; renovated stores; the Bird and Flower Market; a small tailoring shop; steamed dumplings ready for sale; Bai Yun Guan (White Cloud Temple)

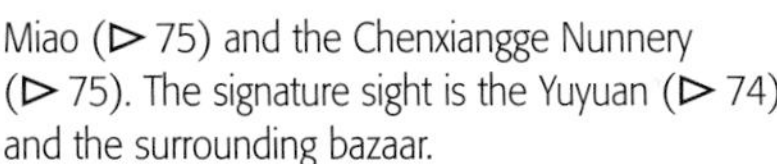

Miao (▷ 75) and the Chenxiangge Nunnery (▷ 75). The signature sight is the Yuyuan (▷ 74) and the surrounding bazaar.

Today The Old Town has been spared much of the over-development that has robbed Shanghai of so much history. Although some rebuilding has taken place, the old Chinese town retains its pre-war atmosphere, stuffed with narrow lanes above which washing is flung out to dry. The disheveled streets are filled with small specialist shops selling walking sticks or tea, and markets overflowing with food, collectibles and knickknacks. There are several antique markets, but you'll need a discerning eye to select genuine items. The Yuyuan Bazaar (▷ 76) brims with colorful shops selling traditional Chinese gift items. A variety of tea houses and restaurants are also at hand for recuperation after sightseeing.

THE BASICS

- H7–J9
- Plenty of restaurants in the area
- Dashijie
- None
- Free

Yuyuan

A willow overhangs a pond in the garden (left); detail of a building (right)

THE BASICS

- J7
- 132 Anren Jie, Old Town
- Daily 8.30–5.30
- Plenty of restaurants nearby, in the Old Town
- 11, 14, 26
- Moderate

HIGHLIGHTS

- Rockeries, bridges and pavilions
- Miniature fish-filled lake and pavilion

TIP

- Yuyuan can be crowded, particularly on summer weekends. Try to visit early in the morning or at lunchtime.

Shanghai does have its surprises. Hidden from casual observation in the heart of the Old Town is one of the finest surviving classical gardens in China.

The Pan family The Yuyuan, or Yu Garden, has a very long history. In its current incarnation it was created in the mid-16th century by a certain Pan Yunduan as an act of filial affection for his father. Pan, a native of Shanghai who had been in public service in Sichuan Province, must have been a wealthy and influential figure in the city, for the garden takes up almost 5ha (12 acres), a large chunk of the Old Town. By the time it was completed in 1577, however, Pan's father had died, and although additions were made to the garden from time to time, it suffered from neglect. Twice in the 19th century it was used as headquarters—in 1842 by the British Land Force and in the 1850s by the Small Swords Society, dedicated to the restoration of the Ming dynasty.

Today's garden The Yu Garden exemplifies the classic Ming garden, where rock gardens, bridges and ponds surround pavilions and corridors to create an illusion of a natural landscape. In reality, although the materials used are the work of nature, the design is very obviously the work of man. But what is important in this garden is the "harmony of scale," its beauty lying in the intricate design, which in the past would have permitted tranquil contemplation in a comparatively small area. An unusual feature is the sculpted dragon that curls around the top of the garden wall.

More to See

BAI YUN GUAN (WHITE CLOUD TEMPLE)

Relocated quite a few years ago from its former location to the west of the Old Town, this Taoist temple is quite modern in feel but is worth a look to compare and contrast with Buddhist temples.

H7 ✉ 239 Dajing Lu 🕒 Daily 9–5 Dashijie Inexpensive

CHENGHUANG MIAO (TEMPLE OF THE CITY GOD)

The Temple of the City God has been reconstructed more than 20 times since it was founded in 1403, but its popularity with devotees, especially those praying for wealth and prosperity, remains undiminished. The hall of the City God is to the rear of the building, beyond the inner courtyard, where you may see red-robed trainee monks, a reminder that this is very much a working temple.

J7 ✉ 24a Fangbang Zhonglu (at Yu Garden) 🕒 Daily 8.30–4.30 Dashijie ♿ None Inexpensive

CHENXIANGGE NUNNERY

This small Buddhist temple belonged to the Pan family, who built Yuyuan. It takes its name from an eaglewood statue of the Buddha, which gives off a resinous scent in damp weather.

J7 ✉ 2a Chenxiangge Lu 🕒 Daily 7–4 11, 24, 26 ♿ None Inexpensive

DAJING PAVILION

The Old Town Wall was felled at the end of the Qing dynasty and this is the last remnant. There is a very small preserved section of battlements, which can be climbed, but it's more interesting as a monument to a vanished era.

H7 ✉ Dajing Lu 🕒 Daily 9–5 Dashijie Inexpensive

DONGJIADU CATHEDRAL

Built by Spanish Jesuits in 1853 as the St. Xavier cathedral, in a style reminiscent of Iberian colonial baroque, Dongjiadu is the oldest Catholic church in Shanghai and stands outside the southeastern edge of the Old Town, a few blocks from the Huangpu

Statue of Confucius at Wen Miao temple (▷ 76)

Worshipers at Chenxiangge Nunnery

River. It is a working church, with Mass in Chinese said daily.
✚ K9 ✉ 175 Dongjiadu Lu Ⓜ Nanpu Bridge ✋ Free

FUYOU MARKET

One of Shanghai's most well-known antiques markets, this place is at its busiest early on Sundays, but there's a permanent collection of stalls here that are open daily. Prices can be quite high, so haggling is a must.
✚ H7 ✉ 459 Fangbang Zhonglu 🕐 Daily 9–5 🍴 Restaurants Ⓜ Laoximen 🚌 11, 14, 26 ♿ None ✋ Free

WEN MIAO

This Confucian Temple is south of the Temple of the City God and not too far from the site of the Old West Gate. It is typical of Confucius temples the land over, with its main hall, the Dacheng Hall, dedicated to the sage. The small number of worshipers points to the decline of Confucianism, relative to Buddhism or Christianity, although the influence of Confucius over all Chinese people is still immense. A used-book market is held in the temple on Sunday mornings.
✚ H8 ✉ 215 Wenmiao Lu 🕐 Daily 8.30–4.30 Ⓜ Laoximen 🚌 11, 14, 26 ♿ None ✋ Inexpensive

XIAOTAOYUAN MOSQUE

Worth a visit to appreciate the multi-religious character of Shanghai, this small mosque was built in 1917.
✚ H8 ✉ 52 Xiaotaoyuan Lu 🕐 Daily 8–7 Ⓜ Laoximen

YUYUAN BAZAAR

Despite appearances—ceremonial gateways, rosewood lanterns, pagodas with sloping eaves—the Yuyuan Bazaar was built in the 1990s. This is one of the best places to shop for souvenirs, though not for genuine antiques. (Haggling is expected, but you may get a better price in the smaller shops on Fangbang Zhonglu.) Stilt walkers, acrobats and street artists entertain the crowds on summer weekends. Rows of stalls sell traditional snacks.
✚ J7 ✉ Streets around Yuyuan 🕐 Daily 7–4 Ⓜ Dashijie 🚌 11, 14, 26 ♿ None

Chops for sale at the Yuyuan Bazaar

The entrance to Yuyuan Bazaar

Old Town

Many old buildings remain in the Nanshi district, Shanghai's formerly walled Old Town, and you will see some of them on this walk.

DISTANCE: 1.5 miles (2.4km) **ALLOW:** 1 hour (not including stops)

START

DONGMEN LU
J8 20, 42, 55, 65

END

FUYOU MARKET
H7 Laoximen

❶ Start at Dongmen Lu, the site of the old east gate to the Chinese town, close to the Huangpu River. Walk westward and pass Waixiangua Jie (Salty Melon Street), with its local street market.

❷ Continue to Zhonghua Lu and cross the street to enter Fangbang Zhonglu.

❸ Continue past a variety of shops until an old Chinese arch appears to the right. This is the entrance to the Temple of the City God (▷ 75).

❹ Go through the arch and make your way among the shops and restaurants until you come to the lake and the Huxinting Tea House (▷ 70–71), near the entrance to the Yuyuan (Yu Garden; ▷ 74).

❺ Bear right around the lake and then turn left to wander among the narrow streets before bearing right to leave this area and emerge into Fuyou Lu.

❻ Turn left here and left again into Jiujiaochang Lu. A street on the right (Chenxiangge Lu) takes you to a small neighborhood temple, the Chenxiangge Nunnery (▷ 75).

❼ Return to Jiujiaochang Lu, walk south to Fangbang Zhonglu and then turn right to browse through the shops of Old Street (▷ 78) and take a peek at the Fuyou Market (▷ 76), busiest on Sundays.

Shopping

DONGTAI LU ANTIQUES MARKET
With its stalls overflowing with Cultural Revolution knickknacks and reproduction antiques, you won't necessarily find anything of great worth here (although you could be lucky), but rummaging through the stalls is endlessly absorbing. It's also a great place to pick up last-minute gifts and souvenirs, but remember this is a tourist market, so haggling is imperative.
G7 Dongtai Lu Daily 9–5 Huangpi Road (S) 13, 42, 63

FRIENDSHIP STORE
While adjusting to competition from nearby department stores, this large branch of the Friendship Store chain continues to sell interesting antiques, including quality porcelain and cloisonné, along with fabrics and craft items. Prices are generally on the expensive side and you can't bargain them down, but many visitors looking for a decent souvenir prefer this approach to the lottery of a street market.
J6 68 Jinling Donglu 6337 3555 Daily 9.30–9.30 Nanjing Road (E) 71

FUMIN SMALL COMMODITIES MARKET
Just outside the Yu Garden, this building houses small shops that sell a wide variety of Chinese products.
J7 223–225 Fuyou Lu Daily 9am–10pm Nanjing Road (E) 11, 14, 26

HONGQIXIANG FABRIC MARKET
The former Dongjiadu has moved around since closing several years ago and recently moved to these indoor premises in the Old Town. There's a large selection of raw textiles to choose from (wool, silk, linen, cotton and others), sold from scores of stalls. You can also have clothes made to measure here, although you may have to hunt around to find someone who speaks English.
J8 168 Dongmen Lu 6330 1043 Daily 8.30–6.30 Nanjing Road (E)

BUYING ANTIQUES

It is illegal to export anything older than 150 years. A red seal on an antique will tell you that it is genuine and exportable. There are so many shops and market stands selling antiques that the seal of approval may be absent, and if it is, there's no surefire method of knowing what you are buying other than to really inspect the object in question. Some imitations are of a very high standard but are often marked on the bottom as being authentic reproductions. This is information the salesperson is unlikely to volunteer, but if you like the item it will still be cheaper than the real thing!

HUABAO BUILDING ANTIQUES MARKET
Housed in the basement of a building close to the Yu Garden, this is one of the city's best sources of antiques.
J7 265 Fangbang Zhonglu Daily 9am–10pm Nanjing Road (E) 42, 64, 86

SHANGHAI OLD STREET
Not nearly as old as its name implies, having been redeveloped as recently as 1999, the eastern segment of Fangbang Zhonglu at least creates a convincing illusion of being old, thanks to its small shops selling antiques, crafts, bric-a-brac and tea.
J7 Fangbang Zhonglu Dashijie

SILK MUSEUM
This emporium on the edge of the Yuyuan Bazaar sells all manner of silk products, from shirts and jackets to quilts and embroidered pyjamas.
J7 125 Jiujiaochang Lu 6355 0308 Daily 9–8 Nanjing Road (E) 11, 14, 26

Restaurants

PRICES

Prices are approximate, based on a 3-course meal for one person.
$$$ more than 250RMB
$$ 100–250RMB
$ under 100RMB

HUXINTING TEA HOUSE ($)

There's nowhere in Shanghai quite like this venerable tea house (▷ 70) for experiencing a taste of Old China, even if popularity has brought in the crowds.
J7 257 Yuyuan Lu 6373 6950 Daily 8.30am–10pm Nanjing Road (E) 11, 14, 26

LAO FANDIAN (SHANGHAI OLD RESTAURANT; $$–$$$)

Something of an institution, this modernized version of an old restaurant (the name means "old restaurant") serves Shanghai dishes (including noodles, and seafood according to the season) and is conveniently situated in the Old Town.
J7 242 Fuyou Lu 6355 2275 Daily lunch, dinner Nanjing Road (E) 11

LU BO LANG ($$)

International movers and shakers, celebrities and ordinary folk alike pile into this signature Old Town traditional eatery on the edge of the Yuyuan lake. Celebrity status has made the Shanghainese food a little touristy and the bills higher, but the experience is worthwhile.
J7 115 Yuyuan Lu 6355 7509 Daily 7am–1am Nanjing Road (E)

NAN XIANG ($–$$)

The best place in the city to try *xiaolongbao* (Shanghai-style steam dumplings). These are stuffed with various fillings: vegetables, crab, pork. All three floors here are usually busy, so be ready to wait for a table.
J7 85 Yuyuan Lu 6355 9999, ext. 1452 Daily lunch, dinner Nanjing Road (E) 11, 14, 26

OLD SHANGHAI TEA HOUSE ($)

Escape the hustle and bustle of the Yuyuan Bazaar to this small island of peace and sanity. The tea house is awash with 1920s memorabilia, with everything from biscuit tins to old telephones. The staff wear long Mandarin gowns or silk *qipaos* and serve the teas on lacquered trays. Snacks of sour plums, muskmelon seeds and quail eggs come with the tea.
J7 385 Fangbang Zhonglu 5382 1202 Daily 8.30–11 42, 64, 86

LOCAL SNACKS

One of the specialties of the region is *Ningbo* or "pigeon egg" dumplings, little balls of sticky rice enclosing a delicious sweet *osmanthus* paste. Another snack is *zhong zhi*, sticky rice with meat wrapped in a lotus leaf. To find these and other delicious snacks, stop in the Old Town—both in the area of the Huxinting Tea House and on the streets around it, where there are many small restaurants and stalls (H6 26).

SONGYUELOU ($)

Dating back to 1910, this is one of Shanghai's best-known vegetarian restaurants, cooking up a range of mock-meat dishes (the traditional way vegetarian food is prepared in China). Dishes are inexpensive, but tasty.
J7 99 Jiujiaochang Lu 6355 3630 Daily 7am–7.30pm Nanjing Road (E)

XIAO SHAOXING ($$)

There's a relaxed atmosphere here, with modern furnishings and gentle live music in the evenings. The menu offers reasonably priced dishes from all over China. Sample the crab and noodles claypot and *yangcen* (fried rice).
J7 96 Sichuan Nanlu 6328 3992 Daily lunch, dinner 126

茶

A rambling district north of Suzhou Creek, Hongkou incorporates the International Concession. It later became a haunt of liberal and revolutionary writers, artists and intellectuals.

Top 25 TOP 25

Tomb of Lu Xun
Hongkou Stadium
Hongkou Football Stadium
Memorial Hall of Lu Xun
Former Residence of Lu Xun
HONGKOU
Duolun Lu Cultural Street
Dongbaoxing Road
Children's Park
Hailun Road
Jiefang Theatre
Huayuan Lu
Tongxin Lu
Yujingpu
Qingyun Lu
Xijiangwan Lu
Dongbaoxing Lu
Zhongxing Lu
Hengbang Lu
Huachang Lu
Zhiliang Lu
Tiantong'an Lu
Baotong Lu
Huangdu Lu
SICHUAN BEILU
Tian'ai Lu
Shanyin Lu
Duolun Lu
Qingyuan Lu
Hailun Lu
Liyang Lu
BAOSHAN LU
Baoyuan Lu
Yongming Lu
Xilu
Changchun Lu
Tianshui Lu
Xingjiaqiao Beilu
Xinxiang Lu
Xinguang Lu
Baochang Lu
Chuangong Lu
Xingjiaqiao Nanlu
Hailun Xilu
SIPING
Qiujiang Zhilu
Dongjiaxing Lu
Liaoning Lu
Luofu Lu
Zhongzhou Lu
Xinguang Lu
Ha'erbin Lu
Jiulong Lu
Dongxinmin Lu
Wujing Lu
Jiangxi Beilu
HAINING LU
WUSONG LU
Emei Lu
Kunshan Lu
Zhapu Lu
Yuhang Lu
Pengze Lu
SICHUAN BEILU
1
2
3
4
5
H
J
K

Lu Xun Park
Heping Park
Linping Road
SIPING LU
ZHOUJIAZUI LU
Quyang Lu
Tianbao Lu
Xilu
Qingyang Lu
Xiangde Lu
Dongjiazhai Lu
Dongshahonggang Lu
Xingang Lu
Tianzhen Lu
Hongguan Lu
Anqin Lu
Shahong Lu
Tiande Lu
Jingdong Lu
Shajing Branch
Linping Beilu
Yangjiabang
Xiangyanqiao Lu
Huiiamuqiao Lu
Zhangjiaxiang Lu
Tianbao
Yucai
Hongzhen Beilie
Linping Lu
Wuhua Lu
Shalinggang
Tongzhou Lu
Gaoyang Lu
Hailun Lu
Hailla'er Lu
Rugao Lu
Yuezhou Lu
Jintian Lu
Xinjian Lu
Dongyuhang Lu
Shangqiu
Zhoujiazui
hanyang Lu
Xi'an
0
400 m
400 yds
L
M

Duolun Lu Cultural Street

HIGHLIGHTS

- *Shikumen* houses
- Shops selling antiques, art and period bric-a-brac
- Bustling modern Chinese character and colonial-period mansions
- Atmospheric cafés

TIP

- The proximity of Duolun Lu and Lu Xun Park to each other and their complementary character should add up to a decent day out in old Hongkou.

This sensitively restored pedestrian street of *shikumen* houses and pebble-dash villas was once the haunt of China's radical writers. Now it is lined with art galleries, curio shops, tea houses and terrace cafés.

Shops If you take Metro line 3 to Dongbaoxing Road, turn right out of the station, then left onto Sichuan Beilu, you will come to Duolun Lu after about five minutes' walk. Many of the shops here specialize in collectibles: Mao badges at No. 183, porcelain at No. 185 and a host of antiques and knickknacks at No. 181. You can get your name painted in either English or Chinese inside a glass snuff bottle at stall No. 3, 120 Duolun Lu. Also, sit with a coffee among movie memorabilia at the Old Film Café (No. 123).

From left to right: Great Virtue Church; a statue of Charlie Chaplin at the Old Film Café; people strolling along Duolun Lu Cultural Street

Culture You can photograph the old brick doorways, the clock tower and the former Great Virtue Church (No. 59), with its intriguing mixture of Chinese and Western styles. The church now houses small craft shops, or you can check out the exhibitions in the Shanghai Duolun Museum of Modern Art.

Literary connections Bronze statues dotted along the street commemorate the coterie of radical liberal and Communist writers who met here in the 1930s, and who, between them, created a new Chinese literature, far removed in spirit from the fossilized tropes of the past. The most famous of them, Lu Xun, had a profound influence on Chinese literature and is still revered today. You can find out more about him by visiting the museum in Lu Xun Park (▷ 86).

THE BASICS

- K2
- South of Lu Xun Park and south of Tian'ai Lu, branching west off Sichuan Beilu
- Dongbaoxing Road
- 4, 9, 18, 21
- Cafés and tea houses

Shanghai Duolun Museum of Modern Art

- www.duolunart.com
- 27 Duolun Lu
- 6587 6902
- Tue–Sun 10–6
- Inexpensive

Lu Xun Park

The boating lake (left); locals playing Chinese chess (right)

THE BASICS

K–L1
146 Jiangwan Lu
Daily 6am–6pm
Snacks sold at stands in the park
Hongkou Stadium
4, 9, 18, 21
None
Inexpensive

HIGHLIGHTS

- Lu Xun's mausoleum and Memorial Hall
- Boating lake

TIP

- Hongkou Stadium adjoins Lu Xun Park on the west side, making it possible to combine a soccer match with a visit to the park.

If you want a window on Shanghai life away from the city center, then try to get to Lu Xun Park, where local people come to find refuge and meet friends away from their crowded housing conditions.

Hongkou Hongkou is the area north of Suzhou Creek (the Wusong River), a large part of which was the former American Concession before it merged with the British Concession in 1863. The accepted date of its foundation is 1848, when a church mission was established here. After the Americans, Hongkou became home to many Japanese, earning the soubriquet of Little Tokyo. Here also was the Mixed Court (administered by a Chinese magistrate and a foreign assessor), the Russian post office and various risqué cabarets.

Lu Xun Lu Xun Park, originally laid out in 1905, has a large lake with rowing boats for hire in the summer. Shrubs and flowers attract butterflies, while the open-air setting draws amateur painters and opera singers. Every autumn there are chrysanthemum shows. Above all, the park is known for its associations with the eminent writer Lu Xun, who lived in Hongkou from 1927 until his death in 1936, and is best known for *The True Story of Ah Q,* which lampoons the Chinese character. His house, at 9 Dalu Xinchun, Sanyin Lu, on a street just outside the park, is open to the public and illustrates what housing was like in the Japanese part of Shanghai. In the park there is a museum dedicated to his life, as well as his mausoleum and his likeness cast in bronze.

Shopping

EUTORIA

Not many shoppers can afford genuine Ming Dynasty porcelain, but a reproduction might be possible. You'll find these here, along with fine modern Jingdezhen vases and other pieces.
K2 Unit 702, 1915 Sichuan Beilu 5696 7878 Dongbaoxing Road 13, 17, 18, 19, 21, 70

GUO CHUN XIANG CURIOSITY SHOP

Some of the objects on sale in this cluttered little shop are antiques, but "collector's items" might be a better way to describe the curios, minor pieces, pop-culture items, Mao badges, toys and Chinese bric-a-brac from as recently as the 1960s.
K2 179–181 Duolun Lu 5696 3948 Dongbaoxing Road 13, 17, 18, 19, 21, 70

QIPU MARKET

Huge clothing market with piles of items at knock-down prices; get your elbows out and haggle hard.
J4 Qipu Lu Daily 9–5 Baoshan Road

SHANGHAI SPRING DEPARTMENT STORE

Shanghai Spring Department Store is a modern six-floor store, at the corner of Wuchang Lu, where prices are significantly less than those in the flagship department stores on Nanjing Lu and Huaihai Zhonglu. It sells food, clothing, consumer electronics, jewelry, and more.
J4 521 Sichuan Beilu 6357 0090 17, 19, 21, 65, 66

Restaurants

PRICES

Prices are approximate, based on a 3-course meal for one person.

$$$	more than 250RMB
$$	100–250RMB
$	under 100RMB

AFANTI RESTAURANT ($)

There are several Uiguir/ Muslim restaurants in town and this is one of the best. Don't be put off by the unimpressive interior. The food—largely grilled lamb—hits the spot. When you have had enough Shanghai food, this is a great place for naan bread, kebabs (*yangrouchuan*) and cuisine from northwest China's Central Asian-Silk Road frontier-land
Off map Tianshan Hotel, 775 Quyang Lu 6555 9604 Chifeng Road

DUCK KING ($–$$)

You don't have to head to Beijing for Peking duck (*beijing kaoya*) and this well-known chain restaurant—competing with Quanjude (▷ 32), Shanghai's other top roast duck restaurant—combines an attractive and brisk atmosphere with some excellent roast fowl. The menu extends to an entire litany of duck recipes.
Off map 2002 Sichuan Beilu 6587 6917 Daily 9am–10pm Dongbaoxing Road

HONG DONG KOREAN RESTAURANT ($$)

This restaurant has a clean-lined, almost Scandinavian look, although diners sit on comfy wicker chairs while enjoying spicy dishes from the peninsula.
K2 239 Duolun Lu 6540 3636 Daily 10–10 Dongbaoxing Road 13, 17, 18, 19, 21, 70

Pudong is a city of 1.5 million people, typified by its skyscrapers, nocturnal neon lights and huge avenues. It sprang up from farmland in less than 20 years, becoming an icon of 21st-century China.

5
6
7
8
9
J
K
BUND SIGHTSEEING TUNNEL
YAN'AN DONGLU TUNNEL
Binjia
Shanghai Natural Wild Insect Kingdom
Fenghe Lu
Shanghai International Convention Centre
Oriental Pearl Tower
China Sex Culture Museum
Lujiazui
Lujiazui Xilu
Super Brand Mall
Riverside Park
PUDO
Shangri La Hotel
Fucheng Lu
Yincheng Xilu
LAN NI DU
Huangpu

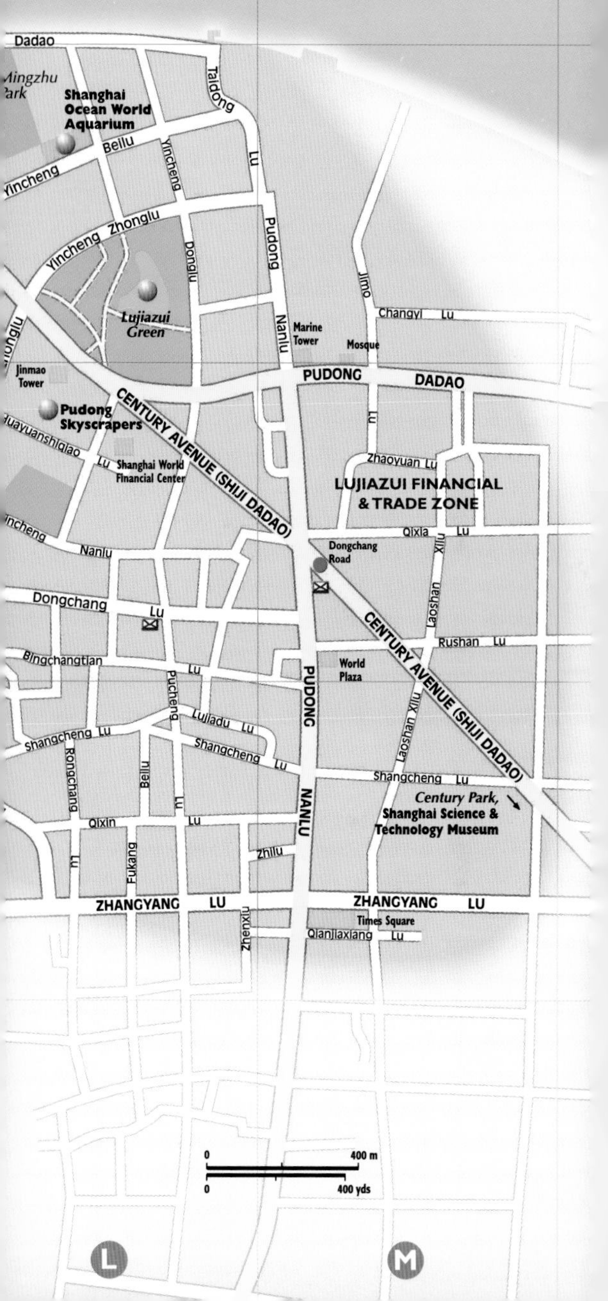

Huangpu
Dadao
Mingzhu Park
Shanghai Ocean World Aquarium
Taidong Lu
Yincheng Beilu
Yincheng Zhonglu
Yincheng Donglu
Pudong Nanlu
Jimo Lu
Lujiazui Green
Changyi Lu
Marine Tower
Mosque
Jinmao Tower
Pudong Skyscrapers
PUDONG DADAO
CENTURY AVENUE (SHIJI DADAO)
Huayuanshiqiao Lu
Shanghai World Financial Center
Zhaoyuan Lu
LUJIAZUI FINANCIAL & TRADE ZONE
Yincheng Nanlu
Qixia Lu
Dongchang Road
Dongchang Lu
Laoshan Xilu
Rushan Lu
Bingchangtian Lu
World Plaza
PUDONG NANLU
Pucheng Lu
Lujiadu Lu
Shangcheng Lu
Rongchang Lu
Beilu
Shangcheng Lu
Century Park, Shanghai Science & Technology Museum
Qixin Lu
Fukang
Zhilu
ZHANGYANG LU
Zhenxilu
Times Square
Qianjiaxiang Lu
0
400 m
0
400 yds
L
M

Oriental Pearl Tower

HIGHLIGHTS

- Spectacular views across the city
- A glimpse into the future of Shanghai

TIP

- There are several other places in Pudong where you can get similar views, including the world's highest observation deck in the Shanghai World Financial Center (▷ 95) or the 88th-floor observation deck of the Jinmao Tower (▷ 94).

The Oriental Pearl Tower rises as a 1990s monument to China's gravity-defying ambitions, and it offers fantastic views across Shanghai. It is emblematic of Lujiazui—the new-fangled forest of high-rises visible across the Huangpu River from the Bund.

Sky-high Towering above the western end of Pudong—two decades ago boggy farmland, now the fastest-growing urban area in the world—the Oriental Pearl Tower is the tallest tower in Asia and the third-loftiest in the world (the third-tallest building, rather than tower, is the Shanghai World Financial Center, ▷ 95). Devoid of any natural grace and typical of the brash early 1990s that sent its concrete form skyward, the tower has nonetheless come to symbolize Shanghai.

Views of the Oriental Pearl Tower, the tallest building in Asia; the expanding city as seen from the tower (below left)

Visiting the tower The panorama over Shanghai and beyond from the viewing area halfway up is excellent. Beyond the views, the highlight of the tower is actually buried away in the basement: the Shanghai History Museum. Take an entertaining voyage through the pages of Shanghai's history, with particular emphasis on Shanghai's rise as a great city under foreign control. Various ticket options are available, such as the Shanghai History Museum alone; the museum plus the middle sphere or all spheres; or the museum plus dinner.

The river A short walk away, the Riverside Promenade is an attractive counterpoint to the tower, with views alongside the Huangpu River across to the historic buildings of the Bund (▷ 58–59). Boat tours are available from the nearby dock situated to the north of the tower.

THE BASICS

K6
Fenghe Lu
5879 1888
Daily 8am–9.30pm
Lujiazui
Bund Sightseeing Tunnel
Ferry from opposite Yan'an Donglu
Moderate
Moderate
Shanghai History Museum
5879 8888
Inexpensive

Pudong Skyscrapers

Pudong's financial district is Asia's fastest-growing. More than 6,000 skyscrapers crowd here, with most of them less than a decade old. The effect is both dwarfing and dazzling, and there are ample opportunities to climb into the clouds for some excellent views.

Jinmao Tower A Chinese pagoda inspired the design of this soaring structure, built by the same firm of architects as the Sears Tower in Chicago, and completed in 1999. It is now the second tallest in China and the fourth tallest in the world, at 1,380ft (420m), and on a clear day there are spectacular views of the metropolis from the observation deck on the 88th floor. To get there, enter from the podium building next door—the elevator will whisk you to the top at a stomach-

HIGHLIGHTS

- Views from the Jinmao Tower's 88th-floor observation deck
- Views from the observation decks of the Shanghai World Financial Center
- Grand Hyatt Hotel's restaurants

TIP

- Pudong's large-scale development is due to be complete by 2010, but further development is likely in the future.

Left to right: The Jinmao Tower, the world's fourth-tallest building; looking down the inside of the Jinmao Tower; a child looking at the view from the observation deck on the 88th floor of the Jinmao Tower

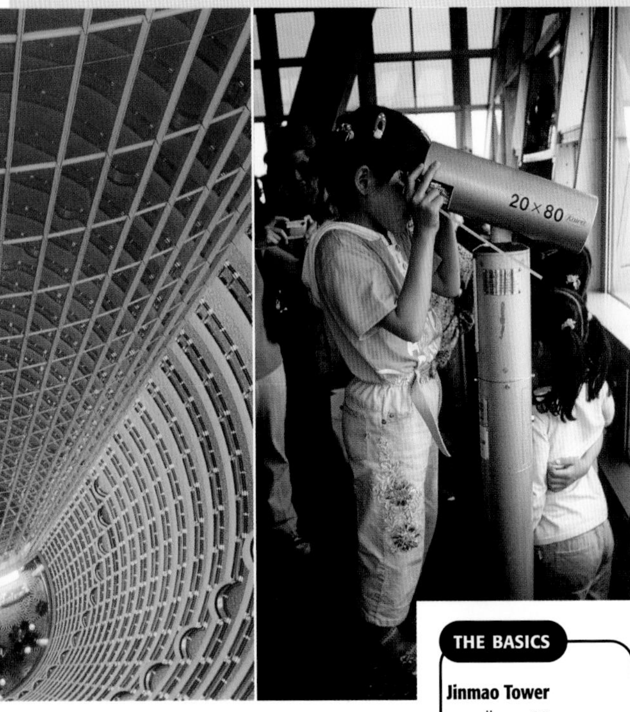

churning 9ft (2.75m) per second. There are retail outlets selling souvenirs, and you can send a postcard direct from the post office. Return after dark when the city is illuminated to enjoy more views and the gourmet restaurants of the Grand Hyatt Hotel (▷ 112), which occupies floors 53 through 87. Cloud 9, on the top floor, claims to be the world's highest bar.

Shanghai World Financial Center With a shape that is reminiscent of a giant bottle opener, this stunning 1,614ft-high (492m) tower is the third-tallest building in the world. It was completed in 2008 and is home to the world's highest hotel, the Park Hyatt Shanghai. There are three observation decks in the SWFC, on the 94th, 97th and 100th floors (the latter is the highest observation deck in the world).

THE BASICS

Jinmao Tower
www.jinmao88.com
L7
2 Shiji Dadao (Century Avenue)
5047 6688
Restaurants and cafés
Lujiazui
Free

Shanghai World Financial Center
http://swfc-shanghai.com
L7
100 Shiji Dadao (Century Avenue)
Restaurants
Lujiazui
Free (charge for observation deck)

More to See

CENTURY PARK

In heavily urbanized Pudong, a park of 346 acres (140ha) is a resource to be grateful for. It has a lake (where you can rent small boats), gardens, pavilions and children's play areas. And a river, the Zhangjiabang, runs through it.
Off map, east of M8 Huamu Lu and Jinxiu Lu 3876 0588 Daily 7–6 (until 5 mid-Nov to mid-Mar) Century Park Good Inexpensive

CHINA SEX CULTURE MUSEUM

This intriguing museum takes a look at the often misunderstood world of Chinese sexuality and culture. It's an eye-opener and gives an offbeat and quirky view of contemporary China.
K6 2789 Riverside Avenue 5888 6000 Mon–Thu 8am–10.30pm, Fri–Sun 8am–10pm Lujiazui Inexpensive

LUJIAZUI GREEN

This large, tree-fringed garden with a lake at its heart is popular with the workers of Pudong's many offices.
L6 Lujiazui Lu 24 hours Lujiazui Good Free

SHANGHAI OCEAN WORLD AQUARIUM

www.sh-aquarium.com
There are 13,000 creatures here. It's the sharks, penguins and spider crabs that draw the crowds, but this is a rare opportunity to see endangered Chinese species. You can walk through the longest glass tunnel in the world (509ft/155m).
L6 158 Yincheng Beilu 5877 9988 Daily 9–6 (until 9 Jul and Aug); animal feeding times around 10.30 and 3 Lujiazui Few Expensive

SHANGHAI SCIENCE AND TECHNOLOGY MUSEUM

www.sstm.org.cn
This state-of-the-art museum, the largest of its kind in Asia, opened to popular acclaim in 2001. The scope of the exhibition extends from biodiversity and space exploration to design innovation and digital technology.
Off map at M8 2000 Shiji Dadao (Century Avenue) 6862 2000 Tue–Sun 9–5.15 Shanghai Science and Technology Museum Few Moderate

The beautiful flower beds at Century Park

Shopping

CHIA TAI DEPARTMENT STORE
This branch of the Thai department store chain, on four floors of the Super Brand Mall, had a shaky start as shoppers were slow to take to Pudong. That has changed now that the store stocks a broader range of goods and as the parent mall has reached a wider target audience.
K6 168 Lujiazui Lu 6887 7888 Daily 10–10 Lujiazui

WAL-MART SUPERCENTER
The US chain store's third branch in Shanghai is at the south end of Pudong's main development zone, close to the approach road to and from the Nanpu Bridge.

SLOW START

Pudong has been slow to take off as a shopping district. This is because shoppers have been slow to change their habits. Now, as more people settle in Pudong, and as the effects of the generally high level of disposable income of people living and working in Pudong have kicked in, the picture is changing. Retailers, large and small, cheap and expensive, are moving in.

Off map at L9 252–262 Linyi Beilu 5094 5881 Daily 9am–10pm Lujiazui

YATAI SHENGHUI SHOPPING CENTRE
In addition to its wide range of modestly priced goods, from clothing to jewelry, the shopping mall below the Metro station at the Shanghai Science and Technology Museum (▷ 96) has developed a reputation as the place to go to buy imitation branded goods.
Off map at M9 2002 Shiji Dadao (Century Avenue) 5094 5881 Daily 10–10 Science and Technology Museum

Restaurants

PRICES

Prices are approximate, based on a 3-course meal for one person.

$$$	more than 250RMB
$$	100–250RMB
$	under 100RMB

DANIELI'S ($$–$$$)
Ultra-urbane Italian cuisine is served in a restaurant with dark, cherrywood decor near the top of the St. Regis Hotel (▷ 112). Look for innovative dishes made with homemade pastas, truffles, porcini mushrooms and more. You can also enjoy some superb views.
Off map at M9 St. Regis Hotel, 889 Dongfang Lu 5050 4567 Daily lunch, dinner Century Avenue

JADE ON 36 ($$$)
This exceptional restaurant, on the 36th floor of the Shangri-La hotel's stunning Tower Two, is a gem of intercontinental, multicultural fusion in a setting of modernist Chinese themes.
K6 Pudong Shangri-La Hotel, 33 Fucheng Lu 6882 3636 Daily 6pm–10.30pm Lujiazui

SHANGHAI UNCLE ($–$$)
The much-loved Shanghai dishes, creatively tweaked with international flavors, have guaranteed the Shanghai Uncle a loyal local following. There are three other branches in the city.
M8 8th floor, Times Square, 500 Zhangyang Lu 5836 7977 Daily 11–3.30, 5–10 Century Avenue

Other attractions lie a little bit farther from the heart of the city, but are still easy to reach and provide another dimension to a trip to Shanghai. With most sights busy on weekends, weekday trips are advised for eluding the crowds.

Taopu
Dacha
20
Jiangqiao
ZHENROU
PUTUO
Jade Budd
Temp
Changfeng Park
Wusong
BEIXINJING
JING'AN
20
Hongqiao Airport
CHANGNING
Shanghai Zoo
SHANGH
9
She Shan, Suzhou, Zhujiajiao
XUHUI
Hongqiao
20
20
Shanghai South Station
Botanical Garden
Huangpu
Hangzhou
20
ZHUHANG
4

Jiangwan
Railway Museum
HONGKOU
ZHABEI
YANGPU
HANGHAI STATION
HUANGPU
Huangpu
LUWAN
NANSHI
PUDONG
Pudong International Airport
Beicai
Chuanyang He
YANGSI
0
3 km
0
2 miles
Yuqiao
Sanlin

Jade Buddha Temple

TOP 25

HIGHLIGHTS

- Active temple
- Beautiful jade carvings

TIPS

- The temple is home to a famous vegetarian restaurant where you can enjoy tasty Chinese Buddhist meat-free dishes. As is the Buddhist way, food is prepared to resemble the texture of meat.
- Photographing either of the jade Buddha statues in the temple is not permitted.

Shanghai's most famous temple stands among high-rise buildings in the north of the city. The highlight of a visit to this small Buddhist shrine is its Jade Buddha in the library and the surrounding atmosphere of veneration and devotion.

The temple The Jade Buddha Temple (Yufo Si) is one of Shanghai's few historic Buddhist temples. It was established in 1882 by a monk from the sacred Buddhist mountain of Putuoshan (the home of the Buddhist Goddess of Mercy), in Zhejiang province, to house the jade figures. Abandoned after the fall of the Qing dynasty in 1911 and then restored between 1918 and 1928, the temple has endured the vicissitudes of the 20th century but has been well preserved. It is certainly not one of China's largest, but is an impressive example of the

Clockwise from top left: Lighting candles from an open flame; a young woman raises a lighted candle; three Buddhas in the temple complex; worshipers at prayer in the temple; dragon detail on the facade; a huge incense burner in the courtyard

South Chinese style, especially the roof of the main hall, with its steeply raised eaves and decorative figurines. The temple is particularly worth visiting on the first and fifth days of each month, holy days that attract many worshipers.

The Jade Buddhas The temple consists of several halls, including the impressive Hall of Heavenly Kings and the ornate Great Treasure Hall, with its three golden Buddhas. The highlights, however, are the two jade statues brought from Burma by Abbott Wei Ken, each carved from a single piece of creamy white jade and separately housed. The first is a 3ft-long (1m) reclining Buddha. The more beautiful figure is in the library; almost 6.5ft (2m) high, it weighs around 2,200 lb (1,000kg), is encrusted with semi-precious stones and emits a divine aura.

THE BASICS

D3
170 Anyuan Lu, Putuo
6266 3668
Daily 8–5
Excellent vegetarian restaurant
24, 105, 106, 112
None
Inexpensive
Regular services

Shanghai Zoo

Residents at the zoo range from birds to the ever-popular pandas

THE BASICS

See Farther Afield map
Hongqiao, Hongqiao Lu (near airport)
Apr–end Sep daily 6am–5pm; Oct–end Mar daily 6.30am–4.30pm
Restaurants
4, 57, 48, 91, 519, 709, 739, 748, 806, 807, 809, 911, 925, 936, 938, 941, 945
Few
Inexpensive

HIGHLIGHTS

- Giant pandas
- Polar bears
- Green lawns
- Play areas for children

In addition to its collection of creatures, Shanghai Zoo is one of the city's most pleasant expanses of greenery and parkland, making it a perfect day out.

Green space This is one of the few parts of Shanghai where you can lie down on the grass in the sun with a soft drink. There's more of a sense of parkland here than at many other of Shanghai's more synthetic "parks." And like most zoos, this is a fun and educational place for children and there are play areas scattered around, as well as a children's zoo. Unfortunately, living quarters for the animals are not the best. The authorities are constantly making improvements, but overall the zoo can hardly rank with large city zoos in Europe or the US. However, the zoo does cooperate with international schemes to preserve rare and endangered species.

Panda stars Needless to say, the pandas—both giant and lesser pandas—are the stars of the show here, and their compound is the best laid-out of all, covering an area of some 1,435sq ft (1,200sq m). It has an indoor and an outdoor area, with a rockery, a pond and trees. But pandas are far from being the zoo's only species. There are some 620 in total, ranging from butterflies to Asian elephants, and coming from all continents. Among them are Brazilian wolves, African chimpanzees, penguins, peacocks, tigers, koala bears, a polar bear, golden-haired and squirrel monkeys, gorillas, South American buffalo and David's deer.

Excursions

HANGZHOU

Within easy reach of Shanghai, Hangzhou is one of China's top tourist destinations and a historic former capital city. It is renowned for its magnificent West Lake.

Most of Hangzhou's sights cluster around the West Lake at the heart of town. Jump on a rental bicycle and circumnavigate the lake; starting at the Mausoleum of Yue Fei and cycling eastward, you'll pass Gushan Island, the Baochu Pagoda (overlooking West Lake from the hills to the north), then cycle south to the Leifeng Pagoda and the Jingci Temple and return via the Su Causeway through the lake itself. You can also take a boat trip to Xiaoying Island and the Mid-Lake Pavilion.

Off in the west is Hangzhou's most famous temple, the magnificent Lingyin Temple, one of Buddhist China's most important shrines. Hangzhou's museums are all free. Make sure you visit the China Silk Museum (in Yuhuangshan Lu) and the China Tea Museum (in Longjing Lu).

Hangzhou's prosperity came from the Grand Canal, which linked south and north China, but the city was also the capital of the Southern Song dynasty. Today it is a green and attractive city.

THE BASICS

Distance: 105 miles (170km)

Off map to southwest

Many restaurants and cafés

Fast trains run to Hangzhou in around 80 minutes from Shanghai South Railway Station

Few facilities

Stay overnight to make the most of your visit. Hangzhou is well-supplied with hotels, from the luxurious Grand Hyatt Regency (28 Hubin Lu, tel 0571-8779 1234) to numerous youth hostels, including the decent Mingtown Youth Hostel (101-11 Nanshan Lu, tel 0571-8791 8948), where you can also rent bicycles

SHE SHAN

She Shan is a hill with an imposing red-brick Catholic church known as "Our Lady of China" at the summit. Mass continues to be celebrated here in Latin.

Its origins go back to the mid-19th century, when a wave of xenophobia led to the construction of a small chapel on the remote hillside. An acting bishop of Shanghai, later forced to take refuge here, vowed that in return for protection he would build a church (the current one dates from 1925). May is a time for pilgrimages, when streams of people climb the hill paths, which represent the Via Dolorosa (the route Jesus took to his crucifixion). Next to the church is an observatory.

THE BASICS

Distance: 19 miles (30km)

Off map to southwest, 6 miles (10km) north of Songjiang town

Train from Guilin Road station (on Metro line 9) direct to She Shan station

Church

5765 1521

Daily 9–5

Restaurants and cafés nearby

Free

SUZHOU

THE BASICS

Distance: 62 miles (100km)
Off map to west
Restaurants and cafés
Regular fast trains take around forty minutes to reach Suzhou from Shanghai Railway Station
Few facilities
Bicycles can be rented at the Mingtown Youth Hostel (28 Pingjiang Lu, tel 0512 6581 6869)

Suzhou is one of China's most well-known canal towns and its gardens are famed across the land.

The attractive Garden of the Master of the Nets (off Shiquan Jie, in the south of town) shows how a compact space can give the illusion of size; the Humble Administrator's Garden (178 Dongbei Jie, in the north of town) is a far larger garden.

Suzhou also has some fabulous temples and pagodas, including the West Garden Temple (Xiyuan Lu), the North Temple Pagoda (Renmin Lu), the Twin Pagodas, the Temple of Mystery (Guanqian Jie) and the Hanshan Temple. The Ruiguang Pagoda, near the Grand Canal in the south of Suzhou, rises up alongside Pan Gate, part of the original city wall.

Suzhou's museums are also excellent. Suzhou Museum (204 Dongbei Jie), designed by I.M. Pei, is visually stunning. Also worth visiting are the Suzhou Silk Museum (2001 Renmin Lu) and the Kunqu Opera Museum (Zhongzhangjia Xiang). If you want to spend the night in Suzhou, there are various options, from youth hostels to five-star hotels.

ZHUJIAJIAO

THE BASICS

Distance: 19 miles (30km)
Off map to southwest
Restaurants and cafés
Regular buses from Shanghai sightseeing bus center at Shanghai Stadium

Zhujiajiao is a small canal town with a wealth of historic features and archetypal images of traditional China.

Although the settlement is much older, it wasn't until the Ming dynasty that Zhujiajiao emerged as a prosperous and well-to-do canal town. Much of the Ming and Qing dynasty layout and architecture survives in the old town and a meander round its alleys turns up countless surprises. The standout sight is the long, hump-backed span of the Fangsheng Bridge, dating from the 16th century. The Yuanjin Buddhist Temple is also fascinating, and worth hunting down is the Catholic Church of Ascension, dating to the mid-19th century. You can also take boat tours along the canal.

Where to Stay

Shanghai has a superb choice of places to stay, from glittering five-star towers to crisply efficient business hotels, fashionable boutique hideaways, low-cost chain hotels and a growing band of youth hostels for the more budget-conscious.

Introduction

While Shanghai is top-heavy with high-end hotels on either side of the Huangpu River, the mid-range and budget brackets are also expanding. Booking ahead is always wise.

Variety of Accommodations

Hotels with historic character are plentiful but are often lacking in international experience. There is a glut of five-star hotels of international quality and a growing band of intimate, fashionable boutique hotels. The English-language skills of staff are generally satisfactory at five-star hotels, but can be lacking even in four-star establishments; staff attitudes can be another problem and the nuances of attentive international service can be curiously absent. There's a mushrooming band of well-located youth hostels, which tend to have young and fluent English-speaking staff and offer inexpensive but comfortable double rooms.

Location

The most fashionable areas are around the Bund, Nanjing Lu, People's Square and the French Concession. Pudong is awash with high-end hotels, but—apart from the excellent views from high-rise hotels—has little charm.

Room Prices

Prices are fast approaching European levels. Book online to secure a good deal. The official rate is hardly ever levied, except perhaps during the May 1 and October 1 holiday periods.

STARS IN THEIR COURSES

The hotel star-rating system employed in China can often be a reliable guide to what you can expect from a hotel, but not always, and may even be misleading in some cases. The nationally determined five-star category generally means what it says, though many hotels that are a decade or two old have never seen any modernization or upgrading, or even a lick of paint, since they were built. Four- and three-star hotels might have been "assisted" to their status by a "sympathetic" local official. Two- and one-star hotels can be surprisingly dowdy and may even have safety issues.

Budget Hotels

PRICES

Expect to pay under 700RMB for a double room per night for a budget hotel.

CAPTAIN HOSTEL

www.captainhostel.com.cn

A few steps from the Bund, the old-timer Captain is still going strong, with clean dorms and a fantastic roof-top bar offering staggering views as you enjoy a drink. Pass on the double rooms, but location-wise, this old sea dog is hard to beat.

J6 37 Fuzhou Lu 6325 5053 Nanjing Road (E)

EAST ASIA HOTEL

In a historic building on Nanjing Donglu, the East Asia Hotel has long been a decent budget standby in the best part of the city. The area can be noisy—this is Nanjing Donglu after all—but you are right at the heart of the action. Check rooms first as they vary and some are noisier than others, depending on which direction they face.

H5 680 Nanjing Donglu 6322 3223 Nanjing Road (E)

ETOUR YOUTH HOSTEL

www.easy-tour.cn

The People's Square perch is fantastic and the main draw, but the historic architecture and courtyard feel of this place are big bonuses. Rooms are clean, but some are on the small side so it's wise to take a peek first.

G6 57 Jiangyin Lu 6327 7766 People's Square

LE TOUR TRAVELER'S REST YOUTH HOSTEL

www.letourshanghai.com

This spacious and well-run youth hostel is quietly buried away down a typical Shanghai alleyway in the Jing'an area. Rooms are pleasant, the staff are friendly, and there's table tennis, bike rental and a room for watching movies.

C5 No. 36, Lane 319, Jiaozhou Lu 6267 1912 Jing'an Temple

MOTEL 168

www.motel168.com

If you're looking for a clean and modern hotel aimed at the lower end of the Chinese business market, chain hotel Motel 168 is excellent value.

Off map 1119 West Yan'an Lu 5117 7777 Jiangsu Road

RESERVATIONS

If you are on a tight budget, it is best not to arrive in Shanghai without a hotel reservation. Budget accommodations are in fairly short supply, and wandering about this huge city with luggage could prove time consuming and expensive.

NEW ASIA HOTEL

www.newasiahotel.com

The location, just north of Suzhou Creek, is excellent and the prices are inexpensive at this art deco hotel, but rooms are rather wanting.

J4 422 Tiantong Lu 6324 2210 Nanjing Road (E)

PARK HOTEL

www.parkhotel.com.cn

The Park Hotel is a classic prewar skyscraper, modernized a little garishly. It has an excellent location and facilities, which include a business area, shopping arcade, beauty salon and several restaurants.

G5 170 Nanjing Xilu 6327 5225 Renmin Park/People's Square 20, 37

SEVENTH HEAVEN

In a distinctive prewar building on Nanjing Lu, Seventh Heaven offers reasonable prices. Rooms are fairly well equipped and hotel facilities include a business center, clinic, post office and a number of restaurants, including Cantonese and Sichuan options.

H5 Nanjing Donglu 6322 0777 People's Square 27

Mid-Range Hotels

PRICES

Expect to pay between 700 and 1,500RMB for a double room per night for a mid-range hotel.

ASTOR HOUSE HOTEL

www.astorhousehotel.com

Astor House offers a taste of concession-era Shanghai, with huge rooms and a sense of grandeur, all within walking distance of the Bund.

K5 15 Huangpu Lu 6324 6388 Nanjing Road (E) 28

BROADWAY MANSIONS HOTEL

www.broadwaymansions.com

Renovated with a crisp new interior, this art deco hotel has a fantastic position, with views of the Huangpu River and Lujiazui, while overlooking Suzhou Creek and Waibaidu Bridge.

K5 20 Suzhou Beilu 6324 6260 Nanjing Road (E)

CENTRAL HOTEL

www.centralhotelshanghai.com

This popular hotel, with WiFi, offers dependable value for visitors who want to be right at the very heart of things.

H5 555 Jiujiang Lu 5396 5000 Nanjing Road (E)

CYPRESS

www.jinjianghotels.com

About 1 mile (2km) from Hongqiao Airport and connected by a free shuttle bus, this modern hotel is in extensive gardens that give a sense of being in the country—you can even fish in a small lake. The rooms are functional but attractive.

Off map 2419 Hongqiao Lu 6268 8868 4, 57, 48, 91

EQUATORIAL HOTEL

www.equatorial.com

High-rise hotel, not far from the western part of Nanjing Lu, with a steak house, Italian, Cantonese and Japanese restaurants, and a 24-hour café. Also a gym, pool, sauna and tennis and squash courts.

C6 65 Yan'an Xilu 6248 1688 Jing'an Temple 71

HENGSHAN PICARDIE HOTEL

www.hengshanhotel.com

Restorations have brought a measure of class back to this art deco hotel—once the Picardie Apartments—on the French Concession edges. Excellent discounts are a further bonus.

B8 534 Hengshan Lu 6437 7050 Hengshan Road

BARGAINS

Hotels in Shanghai are expensive, but don't necessarily go by the official room rate, which hardly ever applies (except during busy holiday periods). Room rates are generally discounted by between 10 and 60 percent, so a hotel with luxury rates could turn out to be a far more affordable mid-range option.

HYATT ON THE BUND

It's not quite on the Bund, but the Hyatt's two towers have great views of the Bund and Pudong. The modern decor is stylish without going overboard, and rooms are spacious and cutting-edge.

K5 199 Huangpu Lu 6393 1234 Nanjing Road (E)

JIN JIANG HOTEL

www.jinjianghotels.com

This art deco French Concession hotel is just off Huaihai Zhonglu, so sightseeing and shopping are a breeze. Rooms are in various buildings, with very different tariffs. There are excellent restaurants on site and nearby.

E7 59 Maoming Nanlu 6258 2582 Shanxi Road (S)

MANSION HOTEL

Former hangout of Green Gang boss Du Yuesheng, the Mansion Hotel conjures up the mood of 1930s Shanghai with its French Concession perch and period styling.

D7 82 Xinle Lu 5403 9888 Shanxi Road (S)

MARRIOTT HONGQIAO

www.marriott.com/shaqi

This family-friendly hotel in a pleasant residential area of west Shanghai offers excellent facilities at

reasonable prices. Handy for Hongqiao Airport, it is also close to the Yan'an Expressway, with fast transit to the center. Rooms are spacious and tastefully furnished, and there's a gym and sauna.
Off map 2270 Hongqiao Lu 6237 6000 911, 925, 936

NEW WORLD MAYFAIR HOTEL

www.newworldmayfair.com
Efficient and neat, this mid-range business hotel offers good views from its north side over Zhongshan Park. Although it's flung off in the west of the city, it's next to Zhongshan Park Metro station for swift access to town on line 2.
Off map 1555 Dingxi Lu 6240 8888 Zhongshan Park

NOVOTEL ATLANTIS

www.novotel.com
While it mimics the typical model of a large, business-oriented tower hotel, its ownership by a French chain affords the Atlantis some refreshing design and service touches. It's a bit isolated, but four restaurants, three bars, a pool and other amenities, including kids' activities, compensate.
Off map 728 Pudong Dadao 5036 6666 Dongchang Road

OLD HOUSE INN

www.oldhouse.com
Be transported back to the Shanghai of the 1930s: Stay in this quaint and beautifully renovated lane house in the French Concession. All 12 rooms are tastefully furnished in Ming-dynasty style with canopy beds, carved wooden cabinets and fine silk drapes. The restaurant serves typical Shanghainese cuisine.
C6 16, Lane 351, Huashan Lu 6248 6118 Jing'an Si

PEACE HOTEL

www.shanghaipeacehotel.com
The classic Shanghai hotel on the Bund, the Peace Hotel's position and historical associations are hard to beat. Facilities include a business center, gym and restaurants.
J5 20 Nanjing Donglu 6321 6888 Closed for renovations until 2010 Nanjing Road (E) 27

LODGING IN PUDONG

Pudong has a virtually complete absence of anything that remotely resembles traditional Chinese style. Twenty-first century Chinese style is something else. The fact that everything is shiny, international and new, and works, makes Pudong attractive in its own right. And it's easy enough to be whisked across the river by taxi, shuttle bus or limousine, or by Metro or ferry, to be back where the action is.

RADISSON HOTEL SHANGHAI NEW WORLD

www.radisson.com/shanghaicn_newworld
Rising over Renmin Park and People's Square, this modern tower—topped with a flying-saucer-style revolving restaurant—offers good value, first-rate views and a host of facilities, plus a high-altitude bar.
G5 88 Nanjing Xilu 6359 9999 People's Square

RUIJIN GUEST HOUSE

Guests stay in five red-brick villas—mostly dating from the 1920s—in the grounds of the former Morris Estate. The setting is simply stunning: Within a walled enclosure are a Japanese garden, a small lake and manicured lawns. The tasteful rooms are a good size; some have balconies overlooking the garden.
E8 118 Ruijin 2-Lu 6472 5222 Shanxi Road (S)

TAIYUAN VILLA

This elegant French-Renaissance-style mansion in a secluded garden formerly belonged to US general George Marshall. Most of the accommodations are in villas around the mansion. The hotel has few facilities, but there are plenty of bars and restaurants nearby.
D8 160 Taiyuan Lu 6471 6688 Hengshan Road

Luxury Hotels

PRICES

Expect to pay more than 1,500RMB per night for a double room.

GRAND HYATT

www.shanghai.grand.hyatt.com

Spectacular views are the preserve of the Hyatt, which takes the top 34 floors of the Jinmao Tower (▷ 94). All rooms have floor-to-ceiling windows, but those facing the river are the most sought-after.

L7 88 Shiji Dadao (Century Avenue) 5049 1234 Lujiazui

JIA

www.jiashanghai.com

The Hong Kong hotel name has come to Shanghai with this hip operation just off Nanjing Lu. In the lobby trendy, tongue-in-cheek design features create a fun and stylish entrée to the uniquely cool rooms.

E5 931 Nanjing Xilu 6217 9000 Nanjing Road (W)

OKURA GARDEN HOTEL SHANGHAI

www.gardenhotelshanghai.com

Close to Huaihai Zhonglu, this hotel sits behind the facade of the old French Club. It has three restaurants, including a Japanese one, a business area and health club.

E7 58 Maoming Nanlu 6415 1111 Shanxi Road (S) 41

PARK HYATT

Even higher than the Grand Hyatt, the latest Hyatt—in the mind-bogglingly tall Shanghai World Financial Center (▷ 95)—opened in 2008. Some question marks have popped up over the service, but in other areas the hotel is first-class.

L7 100 Shiji Dadao (Century Avenue) 6888 1234 Lujiazui

PORTMAN RITZ-CARLTON

www.ritzcarlton.com

This hotel—an intrinsic part of the Shanghai Centre—remains one of the most superior business hotels in Shanghai, in one of the best parts of town. Service, facilities and rooms are all top-notch and the overall presentation is simply excellent.

D5 1376 Nanjing Xilu 6279 8888 Jing'an Temple 20, 37

HOTEL SERVICE

Your hotel will offer one invaluable service apart from providing a room and shelter: Staff will write down your destination in Chinese for you to show to taxi drivers when you go out. Ask the doorman to make sure that the driver knows exactly where you want to go—and don't forget to take the hotel's own namecard with you for the return journey.

PUDI BOUTIQUE HOTEL

This delicious hotel—in the very best part of the French Concession—offers seductive interior design and high levels of service.

F7 99 Yandang Lu 5158 5888 Huangpi Road (S)

SHANGHAI SOFITEL HYLAND

Excellently located, within easy reach of the Bund, the comfortable and stylish Sofitel has had an injection of flair from a recent redesign. It offers good discounts.

H5 505 Nanjing Donglu 6351 5888 Nanjing Road (E)

SHERATON SHANGHAI HONGQIAO HOTEL

www.starwoodhotels.com

This comfortable hotel is convenient for the airport, on the western edge of the city. There are six restaurants, a health club and a business center.

Off map 5 Zunyi Lu 6275 8888 57

ST. REGIS

www.starwoodhotels.com

Regularly voted one of Asia's best hotels, the St. Regis offers the ultimate in luxury and some incredibly spacious standard rooms. Guests have access to their own butler 24 hours a day.

Off map 889 Dongfang Lu 5050 4567 Dongfang Lu

Use this section to help you plan your visit to Shanghai. We have suggested the best ways to get around the city and useful information for when you are there.

Planning Ahead

When to Go

The best time to visit Shanghai is either in late spring (April/May) or in early autumn (late September to October), when days can be clear and warm and comfortable for exploring on foot. June and July are very hot and see occasional epic rainstorms; August is also very hot. Winter is miserable, damp and cold.

TIME

Shanghai is 13 hours ahead of New York and 8 hours ahead of the UK. Shanghai does not have daylight saving.

AVERAGE DAILY MAXIMUM TEMPERATURES

JAN	FEB	MAR	APR	MAY	JUN	JUL	AUG	SEP	OCT	NOV	DEC
45°F	46°F	50°F	64°F	73°F	79°F	88°F	86°F	77°F	72°F	61°F	50°F
7°C	8°C	10°C	18°C	23°C	26°C	31°C	30°C	25°C	22°C	16°C	10°C

Spring (March to May) is a pleasant time. The trees begin to blossom in April; May is usually comfortably warm but is often wet.

Summer (June to August) is extremely hot and humid, particularly July and August.

Autumn (September to October) is often pleasantly warm, although September is also one of the wetter months, and watch out for unexpectedly hot days.

Winter (November to February) is cold, clammy and overcast with occasional snow, but temperatures don't often fall below freezing. It can be an unpleasant time to be in Shanghai.

WHAT'S ON

The dates of traditional Chinese festivals vary from year to year according to the lunar calendar, which usually begins in February.

Winter/spring *Chinese New Year/Spring Festival*: The most important festival in the Chinese calendar usually falls in February. Red envelopes containing money are given to encourage prosperity. It's a festive time to be in the city, but getting tickets for journeys out of town can be tricky.

Lantern Festival (15th day of the first lunar month): Locals eat *tangyuan* (sticky and sweet dumplings), visit temples and may hang out paper lanterns.

Guanyin's Birthday (19th day of the second moon): Guanyin is the goddess of mercy, and on her birthday Buddhist temples are filled with worshipers.

Longhua Temple Fair (third lunar month): Celebrating the founding of Longhua Temple.

May *International Labor Day* (May 1): Three-day holiday.

Music Festival: A festival of classical western and traditional music.

June *Children's Day* (Jun 1).

September *Mid-Autumn Festival* (15th day of the eighth moon): Recalls a 14th-century uprising against the Mongols and is now celebrated with Moon cakes, filled with lotus root, dates and sesame.

October *National Day* (Oct 1): Celebration of the founding of the People's Republic of China. Week-long holiday.

November *Shanghai Marathon*.

December *Christmas Day* (Dec 25): Increasingly a festive event in Shanghai.

Shanghai Online

www.shanghaidaily.com
The English online version of the *Shanghai Daily* presents a somewhat sober style and all the news the government thinks is fit to print. But it contains plenty of useful news, views and information about practical matters.

www.shmag.cn
Online general-interest magazine about Shanghai, with good entertainment and what's on sections, and decent news coverage.

www.shanghai.gov.cn
The official website of the Shanghai Municipality has an extensive English section covering city news and services, travel, leisure and hotels.

www.shanghaihighlights.com
The Shanghai website of tour operator China Highlights. It features many guided-tour and excursion options in the city.

www.shanghaiist.com
One of the city's best general websites, aimed mainly at the young, footloose, fancy-free and ready-to-party.

www.smartshanghai.com
This hip site aims to get you to the coolest parties, raves, dance clubs and other venues where the action is hot and happening.

www.travelchinaguide.com
This comprehensive general China travel website covers cultural issues in Shanghai in reasonable depth, providing decent introductions to places of interest and practical matters. Note that some information is dated.

www.xianzai.com
Shanghai is just one of several Chinese cities for which this site provides entertainment, dining and travel news and information.

USEFUL TRAVEL SITE

www.fodors.com
A complete travel-planning site. You can research prices and weather; book air tickets, cars and rooms; pose questions to fellow travelers; and find links to other sites.

INTERNET CAFÉS

Amid official unease at the freedom internet cafés give users to receive information and opinions–and concerns about young people becoming addicted to chatrooms and games–internet cafés face strict controls and are often shut down. The internet is subjected to censorship and controls in China. You will need your passport in order to get online at internet cafés.

Highland Internet Café
H5 4th floor, Mankedun Square, Nanjing Donglu
24 hours
Nanjing Road (E)

Shanghai Library
C7–B7 1555 Central Huaihai Zhonglu 6445 5555 Daily 9–6
Hengshan Road

Internet Café
A8 1887 Huashan Lu
24 hours Xujiahui

Getting There

AIRPORT TAX

- 50 RMB for domestic flights, 90 RMB for international flights. These taxes are included in the price of air tickets.

ENTRY REQUIREMENTS

- Visitors must hold a valid passport with at least six months' validity.
- Visas for all foreign nationals must be obtained in advance from the nearest Chinese Consulate or Embassy. Tourist visas are generally valid for 30 days but can sometimes be extended in China. Since the run-up to the Beijing Olympics, visas have been more tightly controlled–you may not get the visa you want and extensions may be harder to procure. Allow up to five days for its issue. A passport photograph, completed application form and fee will be required. If in a group, you may be visiting on a group visa.
- In Shanghai, visa extensions are issued by the Public Security Bureau, ✉ 1500 Minsheng Lu, Pudong.
- No vaccinations are required unless you are coming from a yellow fever infected area. However, doctors may recommend certain precautionary measures.

AIRPORTS

International flights arrive at Shanghai Pudong International Airport (PVG), 19 miles (30km) east of the city. Domestic flights use Pudong International Airport or Hongqiao International Airport, in the west of Shanghai.

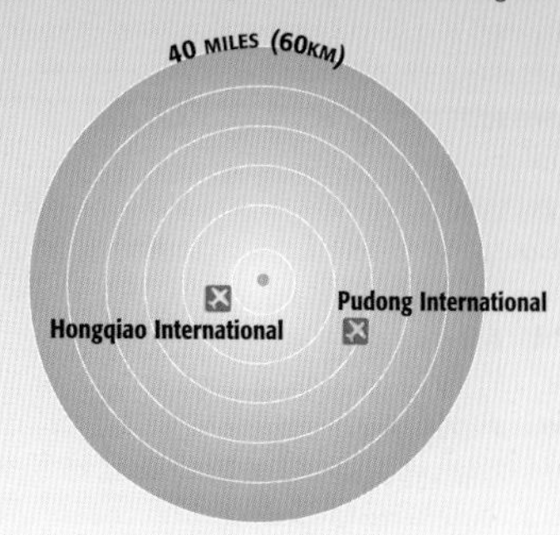

ARRIVING BY AIR (INTERNATIONAL)

The website for Shanghai Pudong International Airport is www.shanghaiairport.com. At the airport, information counters are by the domestic and international security check areas and airside in the domestic departure area. There is a luggage storage facility in International Arrivals (☎ 6834 6078 ⏲ Daily 6am–midnight), as well as ATMs. The airport has a long-distance bus station for buses to Suzhou and Hangzhou. Transportation to Shanghai is by shuttle buses, taxi or Maglev, the world's first commercial Magnetic Levitation rail system. Shuttle buses leave every 10 to 30 minutes from Arrivals; the journey to central Shanghai takes from 40 minutes to an hour or more (seven routes). Buy tickets on board the bus. Taxi stands are to the right outside the Arrivals hall. Have your destination written in Chinese, and ensure the meter is switched on. Ignore the unofficial taxi touts in and just outside the Arrivals hall. A taxi trip will take 25–40 minutes, depending on traffic and your destination. Maglev trains traveling at up to 267mph (430kph) take less than 8 minutes to reach Longyang Road Metro station, on Metro Line 2. Maglev is accessed via level 2.

ARRIVING BY AIR (DOMESTIC)

For information about arriving at Pudong International Airport, ▷ opposite. Some domestic flights arrive at the older and far less efficient Hongqiao Airport, in the western suburbs. Both Arrivals halls at Honqiao have hotel shuttle desks, and outside the halls are bus stops for buses to Shanghai Railway Station, Shanghai Stadium, People's Square, Pudong International Airport and other points. Taxis take 30–40 minutes to travel to the city center.

ARRIVING BY BOAT

Two companies operate services from Japan: The Shanghai Ferry Company, a weekly service from Osaka; and the Japan-China International Ferry Co., a weekly service from Kobe. Crossings take two days; ships dock at the International Passenger Terminal in Hongkou. Most passengers arriving in Shanghai by boat do so on ferries from destinations on the East China Sea (Putuoshan) and the Yangtze River (Wuhan, Chongqing). These dock at the Wusong Passenger Terminal in the north of Shanghai or at Luchaogang in the south.

ARRIVING BY TRAIN

Most trains arrive at Shanghai Railway Station, in the north of town on Jiaotong Lu (some trains, for example from Hangzhou, arrive at Shanghai South Railway Station). Hold onto your ticket until you are out of the terminal. Taxis are readily available or you can hop onto Metro Line 1. If you don't have much luggage, the Metro is a better choice than taking a taxi, especially if you have a long journey. Resist the temptation to find a hotel in the area, as it has no charm. The station itself is large, complicated and swarming with people, so you won't want to hang around. It's easiest to try to book any outward train tickets through your hotel, for a small service charge, but remember to book days ahead. Getting hold of train tickets during the Chinese New Year, the May 1 and October 1 holiday periods can be very tricky.

CUSTOMS REGULATIONS

- You may import 400 cigarettes, 1.5 liters of alcohol, 0.5 liters of perfume.
- When departing, be careful that any antique you have purchased is permitted to leave the country. Antiques that are permitted for export must bear a red seal and any item not carrying the seal may be seized at customs.

VISITORS WITH A DISABILITY

China is not a country that has made many concessions to people with disabilities. However, very slowly, things are improving. As new hotels and museums are constructed, so access is being made easier for wheelchair users and wheelchairs are more readily available at airports. However, attitudes, in general, are not thoughtful or considerate–you should be prepared for difficulties and for the need to improvise.

INSURANCE

- Travel insurance covering medical expenses is essential.
- In the event of medical treatment, be sure to keep all receipts.

Getting Around

MAPS

Tourist maps of Shanghai are widely available from bookshops, hotels and tourist information centers.

WALKING BLUES

While getting around on foot is a great way to see the city, remember that distances are large and the streets are filled with pedestrians, traffic and noise. It can be exhausting, particularly in summer. It makes more sense to go by taxi or public transportation to the general area you want to explore and walk from there. Be cautious at all times when crossing roads, even at traffic lights. Shanghai's drivers show no mercy to mere pedestrians.

TAXI TRIALS

Many taxi drivers are from out of town and have only a superficial knowledge of Shanghai's roads. Take a look at the number of stars below the driver's photo on the dashboard; one is a beginner, five is an expert. Very few drivers speak English well, so have the address of your destination written down in Chinese. Avoid illegal taxis. Well-known taxi companies include Dazhong Taxi (☎ 96822) and Qiangsheng Taxi (☎ 6258 5000).

BICYCLES

- Bicycles (*zixingche*) are widely used and can be rented at little cost from some hotels or from specialist outlets. Bicycles are banned from some large roads in Shanghai, however.
- Check brakes and tires before setting out and observe how traffic functions in China–joining it unprepared can be an unnerving experience.

BUSES

- The comprehensive bus system is very inexpensive but buses can be crowded, especially during rush hour; buses are not foreigner-friendly, unless you can read Chinese.
- Buses run between 5am and 11pm.
- The best tourist bus routes are: the No. 11, which shuttles around the Old Town; the No. 18, which runs between the railway station, Xizang Lu and the river; the No. 20, which travels from the Bund through People's Square to Jing'an Temple; and the No. 65, which runs between the Bund and close to the railway station.
- Make sure that you have small change–you pay your fare on board.
- Note that pushing your way on board is a feature of daily life. Pickpockets are not unknown.

FERRIES

- Ferries cross the Huangpu River between Pudong and the Bund from 7am to 10pm. Single fares are 2RMB.

METRO

- Shanghai's Metro network currently has eight lines, and is now the longest Metro system in China. Still ambitiously expanding, the network is expected to total more than 300 miles (500km) by 2010.
- The busiest station is People's Square, intersected by Lines 1, 2 and 8. Line 1 runs from Fujin Road in the north to Xinzhuang, via Shanghai Railway Station. Line 2 goes east from Songhong Road to Zhangjiang High-

Technology Park in Pudong, via the Maglev station at Longyang Road. Line 3 links North Jiangyang Road with Shanghai South Railway Station. Line 4 runs in a huge loop, linking Puxi and Pudong. Another useful line is Line 8, running from Yaohua Road in Pudong through People's Square to Shiguang Road.

- Trains run every few minutes from 5.30 or 6 in the morning until 10.30 or 11 in the evening, and platform screens show the next two trains due. Signs and announcements are in English and Chinese.
- Fares range from 3RMB to 8RMB. Travel in the central area on Lines 1 and 2 costs from 3RMB to 4RMB. Single tickets can be bought from station concourse vending machines or at ticket windows. For multiple journeys, buy a Shanghai Public Transportation Card, an electronic smart card swiped on automated ticket barriers. Refundable cards costing 30RMB are available from stations and convenience stores and can be topped up as desired. The cards can also be used for buses, taxis and ferries.
- Overcrowding is a problem during rush hours, notably at People's Square. Glass safety screens with sliding doors have been installed on some platform edges.
- Shanghai Metro lines are being renamed. Each line number will be prefixed by a letter identifying it as an elevated light railway (L), a central business district subway (M) or one serving the suburbs (R).

TAXIS

- Taxis are widely available, metered and easy to flag down.
- Travel by taxi is quite inexpensive and definitely the best way of getting around, occasional traffic jams notwithstanding.
- In general, Shanghai taxi drivers are very honest. However, if you are dissatisfied take note of the license number displayed inside.
- Never accept an offer of a ride from a driver of an illegal taxi. There are plenty of legal taxis in the city.

RETURN ADDRESS

Always carry with you a card or handwritten note in Chinese stating your hotel name and address, and perhaps even directions for how to get there if it is not likely to be well known or in an easily identifiable location. This will be particularly useful for taxi drivers—but might also come in handy should you be involved in an accident or lose your wallet or handbag. An extension of this precaution would be to carry information in Chinese about any chronic medical condition you have or medicines you need to take.

SIDE TRIPS

Shanghai is within striking distance of several of China's most interesting small—by Chinese standards—cities: Suzhou (▷ 106; the city of classic Chinese gardens); Hangzhou (▷ 105; described by Marco Polo as paradise on earth); Nanjing (a former capital on the Yangtze, with historical tombs and other sights on forested hills above the river); and Wuxi (the most convenient gateway to Lake Tai/Taihu). All of these can be reached by organized tour, or by train from Shanghai. Have someone at your hotel write down your destination in Chinese.

Essential Facts

EMERGENCY NUMBERS

- Ambulance ☎ 120
- Fire ☎ 119
- Police ☎ 110

MONEY

RMB (Renminbi) is the currency of China. The basic unit is the yuan (often called "kuai" in spoken Chinese), made up of 10 jiao (often called "mao" in spoken Chinese), each of which is divided into 10 fen (rarely used). There are notes for 1, 2, 5, 10, 20, 50 and 100 yuan, and the smaller 1, 2 and 5 jiao. There are also coins for 1 yuan; 1 and 5 jiao; and 5 fen.

20 yuan

50 yuan

100 yuan

ELECTRICITY

- The power supply is 220V, 50 cycles AC.
- Plug types vary, the most common is the two-flat-pin type. It is worth taking an adaptor.

ETIQUETTE

- Avoid displays of anger and aggression. If you have a complaint, gentle, persistent questioning is the best way of dealing with it.
- Remember that China is an authoritarian country where unorthodox opinions are discouraged.
- Table etiquette depends on where you eat. Good table manners are essential in smart restaurants, and especially at banquets, but at cheaper restaurants chicken bones are flung on the floor and a pall of cigarette smoke hangs over loud-talking diners.

MEDICAL TREATMENT

- Treatment is available in state hospitals and in private, joint-venture clinics.
- For minor ailments, the foreigner section of the state-run hospitals will normally be the cheapest option. However, try to ascertain the cost of treatment in advance.
- Your host organization (eg. CITS) or hotel will help to put you in contact with a hospital.
- Private clinics: Shanghai United Family Hospital ✉ 1139 Xianxia Lu ☎ 5133 1900, www.unitedfamilyhospitals.com; World Link Medical Centre ✉ Shanghai Center, 1376 Nanjing Xilu ☎ 6279 7688, www.worldlink-shanghai.com; Sino-Canadian Dental Center ✉ Ninth People's Hospital, 639 Zhizao Julu ☎ 6313 31741, ext. 5276; Shanghai Ko Sei Dental Clinic ✉ 666 Changle Lu ☎ 5404 7000.
- State hospitals: Hua Dong Hospital, Foreigners' Clinic ✉ 221 Yan'an Xilu ☎ 6248 3180, ext. 3106; Huashan Hospital, Foreigners' Clinic ✉ 12 Wulumuqi Zhonglu ☎ 6248 9999, ext. 2351; IMCC in First People's Hospital ✉ 585 Jiulong Lu ☎ 6306 9480; Pediatric Hospital, Foreigners' Clinic ✉ Medical Center of Fudan University, 183 Fenglin Lu ☎ 6404 1990.

MEDICINES

- Western medicines are available but can be expensive. If you have particular medical needs, make sure that you are equipped to satisfy them before you visit China.

MONEY MATTERS

- Money can be changed in most hotels. A passport may be required.
- Credit cards are accepted in international hotels, smart restaurants and tourist shops.
- RMB can be changed back into foreign currency when leaving China but you must produce relevant exchange receipts.

POST OFFICES

- The main post office is on the corner of Suzhou Beilu and Sichuan Beilu.
- Stamps can be purchased from most hotels.
- Post boxes are normally green; but you can hand your mail to the hotel receptionist.

TELEPHONES

- Local and long-distance calls can be made from the plentiful public phone boxes (coins or card) all over the city and from some newspaper kiosks.
- Local calls from hotel rooms are often free. International direct dialing is expensive. International calls can be made more cheaply from one of Shanghai's many telephone bars (*huaba*); phone boxes are more expensive.
- The international access code from China is 00. Or call 108 to get through to a local operator in the country being called, through whom a reverse-charge call can be made.

TIPPING

- Despite official disapproval, tipping is no longer an offense. It is now expected by tourist guides, who usually prefer money—US dollars are popular—to a gift. Hotel porters will usually accept a tip, but there is no need to tip the city's taxi drivers. In most restaurants, tips are not usually expected.

TOILETS

- Western-style toilets are common in hotels and in many restaurants, but traditional squat toilets are also widely used.
- Public toilets are not generally available and those that do exist can be distinctly unsanitary. More and better facilities are gradually appearing but you are advised to carry your own paper and soap.

TOURIST OFFICES

- Shanghai has several Tourist Information and Service Centers dotted about town, but they are of limited use and are often commercially driven. It is frequently best to ask at your hotel for local information; your concierge may equip you with a local map and make recommendations. The following Tourist Information and Service Centers are centrally located:

Nanjing Donglu branch
✉ 562 Nanjing Donglu
☎ 5353 1117 🕒 9.30–8

Jing'an Temple branch
✉ 1699 Nanjing Xilu
☎ 6248 3259 🕒 9–5.30

Old Town branch
✉ 149 Jiujiaochang Lu
☎ 6355 5032 🕒 9–8

Tourist hotline
☎ 6252 0000 🕒 9–8

Language

The official language of China is known as Mandarin in the West, or *putonghua* in China, and is based on the dialect of Beijing. It is spoken throughout China but local dialects are commonly used—the Shanghai dialect is quite different from *putonghua*. However, knowledge of a few *putonghua* words and phrases will undoubtedly be an advantage at some point.

USEFUL WORDS AND PHRASES

GREETINGS	
hello/how are you	*ni hao*
please	*qing*
thank you	*xiexie*
goodbye	*zai jian*
cheers!	*gan bei*
no problem	*mei wen ti*
I'm fine	*wo hen hao*
My surname is…	*wo xing…*
I am from…	*who shi laide…*

IN THE HOTEL	
hotel	*binguan, fandian*
room	*fang jian*
bathroom	*weisheng jian*

POST OFFICES, BANKS AND SHOPS	
post office	*youju*
stamp	*you piao*
postcard	*ming xin pian*
airmail	*hang kong*
letter	*xin*
telephone	*dianhua*
bank	*yin hang*
money exchange	*huan qian chu*
how much?	*Duo shao qian?*
too expensive	*tai gui le*
a little cheaper	*pian yi dian ba*
gift	*li wu*
credit card	*xin yong ka*
antique	*guwu*
silk	*sichou*
jade	*yu*
carpet	*di tan*

EATING OUT	
restaurant	*fan guan, fan dian, can ting*
do you have a menu in English?	*you mei you ying wen cai dan?*
water/cooled	*shui/liang*
boiled water	*kaishui*
coffee	*kafei*
black tea	*hong cha*
beer	*pi jiu*
soft drink	*qi shui*
rice	*mi fan*
fork	*cha zi*
knife	*daozi*
soup	*tang*

GETTING AROUND

bus	*gong gong qi che*
bus station	*qi che zhan*
boat	*chuan*
bicycle	*zixing che*
taxi	*chu zu qi che*
train	*huo che*
toilet	*cesuo*

HEALTH

I feel ill	*wo bu shu fu*
I would like	*wo xiang*
doctor	*yi sheng*
hospital	*yiyuan*
pharmacy	*yaodian*

COLORS

black	*hei se*
brown	*he se*
pink	*fen hong se*
red	*hong se*
orange	*ju se*
yellow	*huang se*
green	*lu se*
blue	*lan se*
purple	*zi se*
white	*bai se*
gold	*jin se*
silver	*yin se*
gray	*hui se*
turquoise	*qian lan se*

DAYS/MONTHS

Monday	*Xing qi yi*	March	*san yue*
Tuesday	*Xing qi er*	April	*si yue*
Wednesday	*Xing qi san*	May	*wu yue*
Thursday	*Xing qi si*	June	*liu yue*
Friday	*Xing qi wu*	July	*qi yue*
Saturday	*Xing qi liu*	August	*ba yue*
Sunday	*Xing qi tian*	September	*jiu yue*
		October	*shi yue*
January	*yi yue*	November	*shi yi yue*
February	*er yue*	December	*shi er yue*

USEFUL WORDS

yes	*shi*	why	*wei shen me*
no	*bu*	who	*shei*
you're welcome	*bu ke qi*	may I/can I	*Wo ke yi/wo neng*
excuse me!	*dui bu qi*	open	*kai*
where	*zai na li*	closed	*guan bi*
here	*zher*	church	*jiao tang*
there	*nar*	museum	*bo wu guan*
when	*shen me shi hou*	monument	*ji nian bei*
		palace	*gong dian*

NUMBERS

0	*ling*	16	*shi liu*
1	*yi*	17	*shi qi*
2	*er*	18	*shi ba*
3	*san*	19	*shi jiu*
4	*si*	20	*er shi*
5	*wu*	21	*er shi yi*
6	*liu*	30	*san shi*
7	*qi*	40	*si shi*
8	*ba*	50	*wu shi*
9	*jiu*	60	*liu shi*
10	*shi*	70	*qi shi*
11	*shi yi*	80	*ba shi*
12	*shi er*	90	*jiu shi*
13	*shi san*	100	*yi bai*
14	*shi si*	1,000	*yi qian*
15	*shi wu*	million	*bai wan*

PRONUNCIATION

The modern phonetic romanized form of Chinese is called "pinyin". It is largely pronounced as written, but note the following:

a as in car
c as in bits when an initial consonant
e as in her
i as in feet unless preceded by c, ch, r, s, sh, z, sh, when it becomes er as in her
j as in gin
o as in ford
q like the ch in chin
s as in simple
u as in oo in cool
w as in wade, though pronounced by some as v
x like the sh in sheep, with the s given greater emphasis
y as in yoyo
z as ds in lids; zh as j in jam

ENGLISH

English is widely spoken in five-star hotels and in places where foreigners congregate. In general, however, you will find that little English is spoken. A major exception is young people, who learn English at school; many of them speak at least a moderate amount of English and a growing number of young professionals are fluent.

Timeline

THE GANGSTERS

Prewar Shanghai was an iniquitous place, fully deserving of its soubriquet as the "whore of the Orient." Nothing illustrates this better than the roles played by the gangsters, Pockmarked Huang (Huang Jinrong) and Big-eared Du (Du Yuesheng), who ran protection rackets, organized drug smuggling and controlled the city's many prostitutes. Du would warn the targets of his protection rackets of the dangers of Shanghai life by delivering a coffin to their door; Huang enjoyed perfect immunity—he was also Chief Detective for the French Sûreté.

Below left to right: Exterior of the Museum of the First Chinese Communist Party Congress; a display in the Shanghai Museum of Chinese History; a bust of Soong Qing-Ling; Mao and revolutionaries on badges at Dongtai Antiques Market; detail of a bronze plaque celebrating the Communist liberation of the city, at the Customs House on the Bund

1300s The trading center of Shanghai becomes a county seat under the jurisdiction of Jiangsu Province.

1553 The people of Shanghai build a city wall during the Ming dynasty (1368–1644) to protect them from Japanese pirates.

1842 The Opium Wars reach Shanghai, which is sacked by the British. The Treaty of Nanking, signed in August, permits them to undertake unlimited trade (Concessions), in Shanghai and four other coastal cities.

1863 The British and American Concessions merge to form the International Settlement; the French Concession remains autonomous. The foreign community enjoys "extraterritoriality," which places it outside Chinese law.

1911 The Qing dynasty falls and China becomes a republic. In 1912, the city walls are demolished to create more space.

1917 Refugees from the Russian Revolution bring a new style to Shanghai entertainment—with outrageous cabarets. Shanghai emerges as the "whore of the Orient."

1927 Chiang Kai Shek is permitted by the foreign community to move troops against the Communists through the Concessions. On April 12, the Nationalists attack the Communists in Zhabei, killing 20 and arresting several hundred, including Zhou En Lai.

1930s Japan occupies Shanghai and remains in power until the end of World War II.

1949 Mao becomes leader of the People's Republic of China and Communist troops enter Shanghai. Few foreigners remain. This is the beginning of the end for the Shanghai of excess.

1966 The Cultural Revolution begins, a period of brutality and terror. Shanghai, China's most industrialized and politically radical city, is the first to enter the fray. Violent rebel groups roam the streets.

1972 The Shanghai Communiqué is signed between China and the US in the Jin Jiang Hotel, signifying the end of China's isolation from the outside world.

1976 Mao dies. The Gang of Four, including Mao's widow, make the city their base in their attempt to seize power.

1990s Shanghai re-enters the industrial world, becoming an autonomous municipality. Pudong is declared a Special Economic Zone, where free trade is allowed.

2008 The colossal Shanghai World Financial Center is completed (▷ 95).

2009 The Waibaidu Bridge (▷ 56–57) is returned to its place at the north end of the Bund after being removed for renovations.

THE GANG OF FOUR

All four members of the so-called Gang of Four, who tried to seize power following the death of Chairman Mao, had Shanghai connections. Jiang Qing, Mao's last wife, was a Shanghai actress. Chang Chun Qiao had been a journalist and director of propaganda in Shanghai. Yao Wen Yuan had been editor of the newspaper *Shanghai Liberation Army Daily*. Wang Hong Wen had been a Shanghai worker and founder member of the Shanghai Workers Revolutionary Headquarters.

WORLD EXPO

In 2002, Shanghai won the competition to host the World Expo in 2010, and it is preparing for its moment in the international spotlight with every bit as much gusto—and with a lot less posturing—as Beijing displayed in getting ready to host the 2008 Olympics.

Index

Shanghai's
25 Best

WRITTEN BY Christopher Knowles
ADDITIONAL WRITING George McDonald
UPDATED BY Donald Bedford
DESIGN WORK Jacqueline Bailey
COVER DESIGN Tigist Getachew
INDEXER Marie Lorimer
IMAGE RETOUCHING AND REPRO Sarah Montgomery and James Tims
EDITORIAL MANAGEMENT Kathryn Glendenning
REVIEWING EDITOR Laura Kidder
SERIES EDITOR Marie-Claire Jefferies

Published in the United Kingdom by AA Publishing

ISBN 978-1-4000-0396-9

THIRD EDITION

IMPORTANT TIP
Time inevitably brings changes, so always confirm prices, travel facts, and other perishable information when it matters. Although Fodor's cannot accept responsibility for errors, you can use this guide in the confidence that we have taken every care to ensure its accuracy.

SPECIAL SALES
This book is available for special discounts for bulk purchases for sales promotions or premiums. Special editions, including personalized covers, excerpts of existing books, and corporate imprints, can be created in large quantities for special needs. For more information, write to Special Markets/Premium Sales, 1745 Broadway, MD 6–2, New York, NY 10019 or email specialmarkets@randomhouse.com.

Color separation by Keenes, Andover, UK
Printed and bound by Leo Paper Products, China
10 9 8 7 6 5 4 3 2 1

A04019
Maps in this title produced from mapping © MAIRDUMONT / Falk Verlag 2010
Transport map © Communicarta Ltd, UK

The Automobile Association would like to thank the following photographers, companies and picture libraries for their assistance in the preparation of this book.

Abbreviations for the picture credits are as follows – (t) top; (b) bottom; (c) centre; (l) left; (r) right; (AA) AA World Travel Library.

1 AA/A Mockford & N Bonetti; **2/3t** AA/G D R Clements; **4/5t** AA/G D R Clements; **4t** AA/G D R Clements; **5** AA/I Morejohn; **6/7t** AA/G D R Clements; **6cl** AA/A Mockford & N Bonetti; **6cc** AA/G D R Clements; **6cr** AA/D Henley; **6bl** AA/A Mockford & N Bonetti; **6bc** AA/A Mockford & N Bonetti; **6br** AA/A Mockford & N Bonetti; **7cl** AA/ G D R Clements; **7ccl** AA/G D R Clements; **7ccr** AA/G D R Clements; **7cr** AA/G D R Clements; **7bl** AA/G D R Clements; **7bc** AA/A Mockford & N Bonetti; **7br** AA/A Mockford & N Bonetti; **8/9t** AA/G D R Clements; **10/1t** AA/ AA/G D R Clements; **10t** AA/G D R Clements; **10b** AA/ G D R Clements; **10/1c** AA/G D R Clements; **10/1b** AA/G D R Clements; **11t** AA/A Mockford & N Bonetti; **11b** AA/G D R Clements; **12/3t** AA/G D R Clements; **13t** AA/A Mockford & N Bonetti; **13ct** AA/ A Mockford & N Bonetti; **13c** AA/A Mockford & N Bonetti; **13bc** AA/C Sawyer; **13b** AA/G D R Clements; **14/5t** AA/G D R Clements; **14t** AA/A Mockford & N Bonetti; **14tc** AA/ A Mockford & N Bonetti; **14bc** AA/A Kouprianoff; **14b** AA/A Mockford & N Bonetti; **15** AA/G D R Clements; **16/7t** AA/G D R Clements; **16t** AA/A Mockford & N Bonetti; **16tc** AA/A Mockford & N Bonetti; **16bc** AA/A Mockford & N Bonetti; **16b** AA/D Henley; **17t** AA/ G D R Clements; **17c** AA/A Mockford & N Bonetti; **17b** ©Robin Whalley/Alamy; **18t** AA/G D R Clements; **18tc** AA/G D R Clements; **18c** AA/G D R Clements; **18cb** AA/ A Mockford & N Bonetti; **18b** AA/A Mockford & N Bonetti; **19(I)** AA/G D R Clements; **19(II)** AA/ A Mockford & N Bonetti; **19(III)** AA/A Mockford & N Bonetti; **19(IV)** AA/G D R Clements; **19(V)** AA/G D R Clements; **19(VI)** AA/A Mockford & N Bonetti; **19(VII)** AA/ G D R Clements; **20/1** AA/G D R Clements; **24l** AA/A Mockford & N Bonetti; **24tr** AA/A Mockford & N Bonetti; **24br** AA/A Mockford & N Bonetti; **25t** D Harper; **25bl** AA/A Mockford & N Bonetti; **25br** AA/A Mockford & N Bonetti; **26l** AA/ G D R Clements; **26c** AA/G D R Clements; **26r** AA/G D R Clements; **27l** AA/G D R Clements; **27r** AA/G D R Clements; **28l** D Harper; **28r** D Harper; **29l** AA/G D R Clements; **29r** AA/G D R Clements; **30t** AA/ A Mockford & N Bonetti; **30bl** AA/A Mockford & N Bonetti; **30br** AA/A Mockford & N Bonetti; **31t** AA/G D R Clements; **31c** AA/A Mockford & N Bonetti; **32** AA/A Mockford & N Bonetti; **33** AA/ A Mockford & N Bonetti; **36l** AA/A Mockford & N Bonetti; **36r** D Harper; **37l** AA/A Mockford & N Bonetti; **37r** AA/A Mockford & N Bonetti; **38l** AA/A Mockford & N Bonetti; **38/9** ©Kevin Foy/Alamy; **39t** ©Tibor Bognar/Alamy; **39bl** ©Kevin Foy/Alamy; **39br** AA/G D R Clements; **40l** AA/A Mockford & N Bonetti; **40r** D Harper; **41l** AA/A Mockford & N Bonetti; **41r** ©Kevin Foy/Alamy; **42l** AA/G D R Clements; **42tr** AA/A Mockford & N Bonetti; **42br** AA/G D R Clements; **43t** AA/ G D R Clements; **43bl** AA/ A Mockford & N Bonetti; **43br** AA/A Mockford & N Bonetti; **44l** AA/A Mockford & N Bonetti; **44r** AA/ A Mockford & N Bonetti; **45t** AA/A Mockford & N Bonetti; **45bl** Photolibrary Group; **45br** AA/G D R Clements; **46** AA/A Mockford & N Bonetti; **47** AA; **48/9** AA/I Morejohn; **50** AA/A Kouprianoff; **51** AA/ A Kouprianoff; **52** AA/A Mockford & N Bonetti; **53** AA/A Mockford & N Bonetti; **56l** ©Robert Harding Picture Library Ltd/ Alamy; **56r** ©Paul Harris/ Onasia.com; **57t** AA/G D R Clements; **57bl** ©Jesper Haynes/Onasia.com; **57br** ©Paul Harris/Onasia.com; **58l** AA/A Mockford & N Bonetti; **58tr** AA/A Mockford & N Bonetti; **58/9b** AA/A Mockford & N Bonetti; **59t** AA/A Mockford & N Bonetti; **59bl** AA/ A Mockford & N Bonetti; **59br** AA/A Mockford & N Bonetti; **60** AA/A Mockford & N Bonetti; **61t** AA/ A Mockford & N Bonetti; **61b** ©LOOK Die Bildagentur der Fotografen GmbH/Alamy; **62l** AA/A Mockford & N Bonetti; **62r** AA/ G D R Clements; **63t** Gavin Hellier/Robert Harding; **63bl** Gavin Hellier/Robert Harding; **63br** AA/A Mockford & N Bonetti; **64** AA/A Mockford & N Bonetti; **65t** AA/G D R Clements; **65c** AA/A Mockford & N Bonetti; **66** AA/A Mockford & N Bonetti; **67** AA/A Mockford & N Bonetti; **70t** AA/G D R Clements; **70b** AA/G D R Clements; **70/1t** AA/G D R Clements; **70/1b** AA/G D R Clements; **71t** AA/G D R Clements; **71b** AA/G D R Clements; **72tl** AA/A Mockford & N Bonetti; **72bl** AA/A Mockford & N Bonetti; **72tr** AA/A Mockford & N Bonetti; **72br** AA/G D R Clements; **73t** AA/ G D R Clements; **73bl** AA/G D R Clements; **73br** AA/A Mockford & N Bonetti; **74l** AA/G D R Clements; **74r** AA/G D R Clements; **75t** AA/A Mockford & N Bonetti; **75bl** AA/ A Mockford & N Bonetti; **75br** AA/ G D R Clements; **76t** AA/A Mockford & N Bonetti; **76bl** AA/ A Mockford & N Bonetti; **76br** AA/ A Mockford & N Bonetti; **77** AA/ A Mockford & N Bonetti; **78t** AA/G D R Clements; **79t** AA/A Mockford & N Bonetti; **80** AA/A Mockford & N Bonetti; **81** AA/G D R Clements; **84l** AA/A Mockford & N Bonetti; **84r** AA/A Mockford & N Bonetti; **85** AA/A Mockford & N Bonetti; **86l** AA/G D R Clements; **86r** AA/G D R Clements; **87t** AA/A Mockford & N Bonetti; **87b** AA/A Mockford & N Bonetti; **88** AA/A Mockford & N Bonetti; **89** AA/A Mockford & N Bonetti; **92t** AA/G D R Clements; **92bl** AA/A Mockford & N Bonetti; 92br AA/G D R Clements; **93l** AA/G D R Clements; **93r** AA/A Mockford & N Bonetti; **94** AA/A Mockford & N Bonetti; **94/5** AA/A Mockford & N Bonetti; **95** AA/A Mockford & N Bonetti; **96t** AA/A Mockford & N Bonetti; **96b** AA/A Mockford & N Bonetti; **97t** AA/G D R Clements; **97b** AA/A Mockford & N Bonetti; **98** AA/A Mockford & N Bonetti; **99** AA/G D R Clements; **102tl** AA/A Kouprianoff; **102tr** AA/A Kouprianoff; **102bl** AA/G D R Clements; **102br** AA/G D R Clements; **103t** AA/G D R Clements; **103b** AA/A Kouprianoff; **104l** AA/G D R Clements; **104r** AA/G D R Clements; **105t** Panoramic Images/ Robert Harding; **106** Panoramic Images/Robert Harding; **107** AA/A Mockford & N Bonetti; **108/9t** AA/ C Sawyer; **108tr** AA/A Mockford & N Bonetti; **108tcr** AA; **108cbr** AA/G D R Clements; **108br** AA/G D R Clements; **110/1** AA/C Sawyer; **112** AA/C Sawyer; **113** AA/A Mockford & N Bonetti; **114/5** AA/ A Mockford & N Bonetti; **116/7t** AA/A Mockford & N Bonetti; **118/9t** AA/A Mockford & N Bonetti; **120/1t** AA/A Mockford & N Bonetti; **122/3t** AA/A Mockford & N Bonetti; **124/5t** AA/A Mockford & N Bonetti; **124bl** AA/A Mockford & N Bonetti; **124br** AA/G D R Clements; **125bl** AA/G D R Clements; **125bc** AA/A Mockford & N Bonetti; **125br** AA/A Mockford & N Bonetti.

Every effort has been made to trace the copyright holders, and we apologise in advance for any accidental errors. We would be happy to apply the corrections in the following edition of this publication.